Competing in Financial Markets

Competing in Financial Markets

How to Trade With the Best of Them

Philip Cooper

BEP BUSINESS EXPERT PRESS

Competing in Financial Markets: How to Play With the Best of Them
Copyright © Business Expert Press, LLC, 2018.

First published in 2018 by
Business Expert Press, LLC
222 East 46th Street, New York, NY 10017
www.businessexpertpress.com

ISBN-13: 978-1-63157-700-0 (paperback)
ISBN-13: 978-1-63157-699-7 (e-book)

Business Expert Press Finance and Financial Management Collection

Collection ISSN: 2331-0049 (print)
Collection ISSN: 2331-0057 (electronic)

Cover and interior design by S4Carlisle Publishing Services
Private Ltd., Chennai, India

First edition: 2018

10 9 8 7 6 5 4 3 2 1

Printed in the United States of America.

Dedication

This book is dedicated to my son Sammy Burton-Cooper who has had exceptional patience with me over the years.

Abstract

Competing in the financial markets will give both the novice and intermediate traders alike a comprehensive understanding of how to trade in the financial markets without losing their shirts. It is primarily aimed at the undergraduate whose ambition is to either become a trader in a financial organization or trade online through a financial brokers trading platform. The book provides seasoned online traders with new insights into financial assets other than currencies. In simple-to-understand concise language, enhanced by relevant graphics, all the key trading tools available for traders are explained in enough detail that novice traders should be able to understand and learn how to trade effectively in the financial markets. Chapter by chapter, this book builds a comprehensive understanding of the basic building blocks of trading assets, covering key charting and technical tools including fundamental analysis and the key economic events. This book exposes the myth that trading is an unfathomable mystery.

Keywords

Candlestick Charts, CFD, Derivatives, Financial Markets, Forex, Fundamental Analysis, Options, Stocks, Technical Analysis, Trading

Contents

Acknowledgments

I wish to express gratitude to Nigel Wyatt of the Magenta Network for offering me the opportunity to write this book. Also to Craig Abbott for his inspiration, which started me down this writing road.

My thanks to ex-colleagues who kindly edited the book for content: Forrest Collier, David Evans, and Roger Francis. Many thanks for your time, guys.

Finally, gratitude to my partner Susan, who did not complain when I went missing for hours on end and who was also my own personal grammatical editor who took a rough piece of work and made it flow.

Introduction

This book will give both the novice and semi-experienced traders alike a comprehensive understanding of how to trade in the financial markets without losing their shirts. I have primarily aimed at the undergraduate whose ambition it is to become a trader, either in a financial organization's trading room or treasury department, or to trade online through a financial broker's trading platform. The book provides seasoned online traders with new insights into financial assets other than currencies. In simple-to-understand concise language, enhanced by relevant graphics, all the key trading tools available for traders are explained in enough detail that novice traders should be able to understand and learn how to trade effectively in the financial markets. Competing in the financial markets builds chapter by chapter a comprehensive understanding of the basic building blocks of trading financial assets. It fully covers the key charting and technical tools, as well as a good grasp of fundamental analysis and the key economic events that affect the markets. The characteristics of all tradable financial assets – currencies, stocks, indices, commodities, and options – are covered with examples and strategies on how to use them effectively. This book exposes the myth that the financial markets are an unfathomable mystery, and I have used my 30 years' experience as an investment banker to cut through the noise and provide a sharpened view of how the financial markets should be traded.

CHAPTER 1

Forex Fundamentals

This book is full of helpful hints, tips, and examples to provide you with enough skills and knowledge to get started in trading financial assets. Trading is a multifaceted business and for those who believe that to make a lot of money all you need to do is read a couple of newspapers and learn to recognize a couple of charts, think again, it is not that easy. Trading is about buying and selling assets, and the critical tenant to making a profit is to buy low and sell high. This does not sound complicated, does it? However, there are issues that you need to think about to be successful in what can be a very risky market. To be a successful trader in the world's financial markets, you need first and foremost to have a good trading education.

A good place to start is at a business school. Most business schools in Europe and the United States have courses which specialize in trading the financial markets. These classes offer a wannabe trader the opportunity to achieve the skills and the knowledge necessary to start trading in earnest in the foreign exchange market. The schools customarily cover all the technical analysis skills and other knowledge such as charting, as well as the economic issues related to fundamental analysis. Knowing how to read the trading signals from a chart is one of the most vital skills a trader can acquire and will maximize the opportunity for earning a lot of money.

Choose a school that offers simulated trading using dummy trading accounts. No matter how good the teacher is and how well you understand what you have been taught, there is nothing like experiencing the real thing, so practicing trading on a simulated trading platform is an extremely important part of a trader's education. Some schools which are well funded even allow their students to trade on a live forex mini-account. These mini-accounts can be funded for as little as USD25, so there is no risk of losing a lot of money. However, it does allow you to experience the emotions and the excitement of the real trading world which is something that a simulated trading station cannot give you.

If after graduating from a business school, you become a professional trader working in a large trading room of a financial institution, you will be provided with further education by the institution. If you become a retail trader and trade from the comfort of your own home, you can obtain further education through reading the appropriate books, like the one you are reading now, or through attending the numerous online web seminars that most online broker firms offer for their customers who have opened an online trading account, even if it is just a dummy account. The knowledge a trader needs is so vast and ongoing that you should probably do all the things mentioned above. When trading, it is better to be fully educated rather than undereducated, so attending seminars and reading books on trading should become part of your ongoing trading strategy.

In the first four chapters of this book, we are going to concentrate on the trading and analytical tools which you will need to master to enable you to trade foreign currencies successfully. These same tools are transferable for trading other asset classes too; these will be discussed from Chapter 5 onward.

Before we discuss the fundamentals of the foreign exchange markets, we should take a brief look at the history of money and currency exchange, from barter to the era of the current financial markets.

History of Money and Currency Exchange

Prior to money becoming the official standard of exchange, people exchanged goods and services through a barter system—the exchange of goods for other goods. This system had important disadvantages in that to be efficient, wants must be matched to needs, and there needed to be a common measurement of value. There was no medium such as a specific weight of gold to measure value, so it was impossible to agree on what, for example, a donkey was worth. Was it a sack of potatoes, or a bag of flour, or several loaves of bread? No one knew, so it was up to every individual to assess a value for themselves. It was not until the establishment of paper money and a set of standard characteristics for money in all countries was introduced that a refined international commerce system could be developed.

Early examples of money were gold and silver coins, and when paper money began circulating it was backed by the concept that the holder of paper could at any time request convertibility into gold. This was difficult to regulate because as more gold mines were discovered and more gold came into circulation, the price of gold would fluctuate wildly with the vagaries of supply and demand. However, in 1875, the official gold standard was introduced. If a dollar-holder found that his dollar-holdings were falling in value, he could exchange them for gold and essentially reduce the number of dollars in circulation, which in turn stabilized the dollar and caused it to appreciate. The exchange into gold from dollars was then reversed. So, by the end of the 19th century, most countries had pegged the value of their currency to an ounce of gold and the difference between the price of an ounce of gold in one country and another country was the exchange rate. Although the gold standard seemed and sounded ideal, nevertheless it ended in the 1930s because the huge expense of the European and American war effort demanded more money to be printed, and eventually, there was not enough gold around to exchange it for the money in circulation. Between the wars, gold made a minor comeback but by the time World War II broke out most countries had abandoned gold once again.

At Bretton Woods in 1944, a new international monetary system was established. This system set a gold-based value for both the dollar and the British Pound while linking all other currencies to the dollar. Gold was set at USD35 an ounce, and the International Monetary Fund was founded with a purpose to help member countries who needed monetary assistance. At the same time, The World Bank and the International Trade Organization (later the World Trade Organization) were also founded. As economies grew after the war, the supply of dollars in Europe was soon worth more than the amount of gold in the United States.

In 1965, the euro dollar market was formed. Euro dollars were dollars held by non-U.S. banks outside the United States, therefore they were not regulated by the United States. As these dollars were not regulated, they bore a higher-risk premium and a higher yield than domestic dollars. It was from this liquid market that foreign exchange forwards and foreign exchange swaps were born.

In the late 1960s, due to the pressure on the dollar, convertibility into gold was suspended and the German Mark revalued against the dollar. Later, the price of gold was again fixed but this time at USD38 per ounce. In 1970, the dollar was under immense pressure again due to the cost of the Vietnam War. Finally, in 1971 the gold standard was abandoned for good. The Bretton Woods system had finally collapsed and the dollar would freely float against other currencies. The ending of fixed exchange rates heralded in the era of floating exchange rates. With it came the European Monetary System (EMS), formed in 1979, where European currencies were floated in a tight band against the dollar and eventually the introduction of the single currency, the euro, in 1999. Without fixed exchange rates, the currency markets have become volatile between periods of relative calm. Foreign exchange trading is nourished by these periods of volatility because it is only under these conditions that you can make money. This book is designed to help you do just that.

Trading in the foreign exchange market is very different from trading in regulated exchanges such as stock, futures, or options exchanges. There are no clearing houses where trades are guaranteed and there is no mechanism for adjudicating disputes. The forex market is a network of thousands of traders sitting in the mammoth trading rooms of the global international banks, whose market share is 51 percent of total daily volume and the trading rooms of global corporations, both of which operate in the world's financial centers. In addition, there is a network of hundreds of thousands of retail traders, trading from their laptops at home, maybe such as you are right now.

The foreign exchange market is open 24 hours a day, except for Saturdays, Sundays, and bank holidays. In other words, it is open from 22:00 GMT on Sunday (Sydney) and closes at 22:00 GMT (New York) on Friday.

It is the biggest, most liquid, and self-regulated market in the world, where business is done on a metaphorical handshake and the global volume is on average USD6.5 trillion a day. The biggest volume is being traded in London where they have a 40 percent share of the daily volume. It is not one market, it is made up of many markets which are situated around the world in various time zones. These markets are connected to one another by very sophisticated electronic communication networks so

Table 1.1 Daily average volume of forex transactions by financial center

Financial center	Daily volume in billions	Percent share
London	2,426	37.3
New York	1,272	19.6
Singapore	517	7.9
Hong Kong	437	6.7
Tokyo	399	6.1
Paris	181	2.8
Others	1.300	19.6

Source: Triennial Central Bank Survey of foreign exchange and OTC derivatives markets in 2016.

that an exchange rate quoted in Tokyo is transparent to market participants in both Europe and America (Table 1.1).

The forex market is open 24 hours a day because it spans three major time zones: The European time zone, the American time zone, and the Far Eastern time zone. If a market in any one of these time zones is operational, a trader sitting in another time zone can trade currencies.

The largest foreign exchange market centers in the world is London, which trades the highest daily volume, followed by New York, and then Singapore which is the third largest. Other big centers in Europe are Frankfurt, Paris, and Amsterdam. In the United States, the biggest centers are New York and Chicago, while in the Far East, Hong Kong, Singapore, Tokyo, and Sydney are the main forex centers.

Unlike American or European stocks which you are unable to trade when their stock exchanges are closed, the dollar does not cease to be traded simply because the New York forex market has closed, it will continue to be traded in the Far East and then on into Europe. There is an actual order of center openings. The first forex center to open is Australasia, followed by Tokyo, Hong Kong, Singapore, all of which are in the Far Eastern time zone. Then, Europe opens and London center starts trading just before the Far Eastern time zone has closed. Lastly, New York opens at 1 p.m. London time and the two trading centers overlap for about 4 hours. Just before New York closes, the Far Eastern markets are already starting to trade in the following day.

Quoting an Exchange Rate

The first thing a fledgling trader must understand is the jargon used in trading, especially the terminology used in the actual exchange rate itself. A trader needs to understand and recognize each component part of an exchange rate.

A quoted exchange rate—(1.5815/1.5820) – is made up of four main components.

The first component is called the big figure and this is the number before the decimal point. The second component is the basis points or pips as they are called. These are the numbers which come after the decimal point. Most exchange rates are just like the GBP/USD, and are quoted to four decimal places like this (1.5815/1.5820) with the final decimal place being 1/100th of 1 percent. Therefore, the smallest change to an exchange rate is one pip or one basis point. If, for example, you purchased 1 million sterling against the dollar at a rate of 1.5820, each one pip change would be $1,000,000 \times 0.0001 = 100$ sterling. The only exception to this rule is the Japanese Yen which is quoted to only two decimal places like this USD/JPY 98.40. A rate denotes how many units of a currency are in 1 unit of the base currency. Therefore, a rate of GBP/USD 1.5820 denotes that for every pound sterling there are USD1.5820.

The currency pair–currency code designation always shows the base currency first and the base currency is always quoted as one unit equaling so many units of the counter currency in the currency pair (Table 1.2).

The third and fourth components are the bid side and the offer side. The bid side of an exchange rate is the left-hand rate which in our GBP/USD example of 1.5815/1.5820 is 1.5815. This is the rate that a bank trader or a broker quoting the rate buys the base currency and sells the counter currency. So, you as a trader being quoted that rate would sell

Table 1.2 Base currency designations

Currency pairs	Base currency	Counter currency
GBP/USD	GBP	USD
USD/CHF	USD	CHF
EUR/USD	EUR	USD
AUD/USD	AUD	USD

sterling at 1.5815, the base currency, and buy dollars, the counter currency. The offer side of the rate is the right-hand side of the rate which in our example is 1.5820 and is the rate at which the person that quotes the rate sells the base currency. Therefore, you as a trader receiving the quote would buy sterling, the base currency, at the offer rate of 1.5620 and sell the USD, the counter currency.

Let us see how this works with a trade. Let us imagine that you believe the euro will appreciate over the next few days. This morning, the EUR/USD currency pair is being quoted at 1.0538/1.0540. You decide to buy EUR5,000,000 and sell the equivalent in dollars, at the quoted offer rate of 1.0540. Following is your position (Table 1.3).

Your current position is showing a USD1,000 loss (each pip movement is worth 5,000,000 × 0.0001 = USD500) because you must sell the euro at the current market bid rate of 1.5038 which is two pips less than you bought the sterling. However, by mid-morning the EUR/USD rate was being quoted at 1.0542/1.0544, in other words, the euro had appreciated by four pips on the bid side and on the offer side. So, if you decide at that moment to sell the 5 million euro you had bought earlier, you would have to sell at the quoted bid rate of 1.0542. Your position is now as given.

As Table 1.4 shows, you sold your EUR5,000,000 at the market bid rate of 1.0542 and received USD5,271,000, that is, USD1,000 more than you had paid for the 5 million euro you had bought early. Hence, you have made a profit of USD1,000 on the trade.

Creating a short position is exactly the opposite of a long position. An investor/trader sells a base currency which they believe is going to

Table 1.3 Long position

Trade	Rate	Long EUR	Short USD	P/L USD
Buy	1.0538/1.0540	5,000,000	5,270,000	−1,000

Table 1.4 Squared position

Trade	Rate	EUR	USD	P/L USD
Buy	1.0538/1.0540	+5,000,000	−5,270,000	−1,000
Sell	1.0542/1.0544	−5,000,000	+5,271,000	+1,000

Table 1.5 Short position

Trade	Rate	EUR	USD	P/L USD
Sell	1.0530/1.0532	−4,000,000	+4,212,000	−1,000

Table 1.6 Squared position

Trade	Rate	EUR	USD	P/L USD
Sell	1.0530/1.0532	−4,000,000	+4,212,000	−1,000
Buy	1.0524/1.0526	+4,000,000	−4,210,400	+1,600

lose value over the short- or the long term. If the base currency decreases in value, the investor/trader can buy it back more cheaply than when they sold it. For example, you believe that the euro is going to depreciate against the dollar. The EUR/USD rate is 1.0530/1.0532, so you sell EUR4,000,000 at 1.5030, the market bid rate. Your position is now (Table 1.5).

Now you are hoping that the market offer rate drops below 1.5030, so when you buy the euro back, it will be cheaper. Later, the EUR/USD rate has moved to 1.0524/1.0526 which is a depreciation of six pips on the both bid and offer side. You immediately buy back your 4 million euro at the market offer rate of 1.0526. Your position now looks like this (Table 1.6).

You have bought back your 4 million euro at 1.0526 in exchange for 1,600 fewer dollars than you originally received when you sold the euro, so making a profit of USD1,600 on the trade. So far you have made two winning trades; however, there has never been a trader or investor who has bettered a 60 percent winning trade ratio consistently. Later in this chapter we shall discuss the discipline and psychology of a typical successful trader, someone who not only manages the wins but also the losses.

Types of Orders

A trade is made up of two separate orders: a buy order and a sell order, and any one of them can be used to enter a trade or to exit a trade. There are at times however different types of orders to facilitate the exit of a trade. If you have entered a trade with a buy order, then the trade will be exited with a sell order. The opposite is true if you enter a trade with a sell order. You will exit the trade with a buy order. As we have just seen in the previous section, if you felt that the market in a currency pair is appreciating, you would transact one buy order to enter the trade and one sell order to exit the trade. Or, if you felt the market would go down, you would execute a sell order to enter the trade and a buy order to exit the trade.

There are several types of orders that you can use in a variety of permutations to make your trades. The most common orders that traders use are as follows.

Market orders are orders to buy or sell a contract at the most recent best price, whatever that price is. In a lively market, market orders will always be executed, although not necessarily at the precise price that the trader wanted.

Limit orders are orders to sell or buy a contract at the exact price or at a price better than the specific price. It depends on where the market is moving whether an order gets filled. However, if they are filled, it will always be at the chosen price or at a better price than the chosen price.

Stop orders are orders to buy or sell a currency at the best obtainable price, but they are only executed if the market reaches the price stated by the trader. When or if the trigger price is reached, the order will always be filled although not automatically at the exact price the trader wanted. Stop orders are triggered when the market trades at the trigger price or when it has moved past the trigger price. Later in this book, we will discuss in detail when it is appropriate to use the various types of orders described above.

Lots

Currencies are traded in four different lot sizes (Table 1.7).

As we know from an earlier discussion, the change in currency values relative to another currency is measured in pips. One pip is a very small percentage of a unit of currency, so to take advantage of this small variation you will want to trade big amounts of a certain currency to gain any noteworthy profit or loss. Let us look at an example of using a 100,000 unit (standard) lot size. In Table 1.8 we can see how much a one pip change in value is worth.

Table 1.7 Lot sizes

Lot type	Lot size
Standard	100,000
Mini	10,000
Micro	1,000
Nano	100

Table 1.8 Value of one pip change in dollars

Currency pair	Rate	Pips	Units	Value per pip
USD/JPY	118.80	0.01/118.80	×100,000	USD8.42
GBP/USD	1.2340	0.0001/1.2340	×100,000 × 1.2340	USD10
EUR/USD	1.0550	0.0001/1.0550	×100,000 × 1.0550	USD10
USD/CHF	1.0150	0.0001/1.0150	×100,000 × 1.0150	USD10

Table 1.9 Value of one pip change in various lot sizes

Lots size	One pip value
Standard	USD10
Micro	USD1
Mini	USD0.10
Nano	USD0.01

As you can see from Table 1.8, where the base currency is not the dollar, we need to convert the final pip value into dollars. Now we know that each pip movement in a standard lot is USD10, it is easy to work out the value of one pip movement for mini, micro, and nano lots—simply divide by 10 (Table 1.9).

Your broker may workout the pip values slightly differently, however whichever method they use the result is near enough the same as shown in Table 1.9.

Leverage

Leverage is when the trader trades currencies with money which essentially has been borrowed from the broker. Foreign exchange brokers offer

Table 1.10 Minimum margin requirements in broker account

Leverage ratio	Minimum margin requirement	Balance in broker account	Minimum margin amount	Equivalent traded amount
200:1	0.50%	USD1,000	USD5	USD200,000
100:1	1%	USD1,000	USD10	USD100,000
50:1	2%	USD1,000	USD200	USD50,000
10:1	10%	USD1,000	USD100	USD10,000

investors leverages of 50:1, 100:1, or 200:1, and some brokers' even offer 400:1. At a leverage of 100:1, you can make a trade (buy or sell a currency) which is 100 times greater than the money you are investing as capital for the trade. This particularly facilitates the small investor who has opened a micro foreign exchange account with the broker but also bigger investors as they can trade in bigger amounts than the capital in their broker accounts. The broker will necessitate you to have a specified amount left in your account after a trade. This is the broker's margin requirement. So, if, for example, you have USD50 in your broker account, you cannot trade the whole amount because if the leverage is 100:1 the broker will require you to have at least a balance of 1 percent of your outstanding trade. So, the maximum amount you can trade is USD49.50. If you are losing money on the trade and your equity has fallen below the margin requirement threshold, you must replenish your account or the broker will close out the trade. Table 1.10 details the margin requirements at different leverage levels assuming you have USD1,000 in your broker account.

As a trader, it is important that you understand both the benefits, and the pitfalls, of trading with leverage. Using a ratio of 50:1 as an example means that it is possible to enter a trade for up to USD50 for every dollar in your account. So, with as little as USD1,000 of margin available in your account you can trade up to 50,000 at that leverage. So, you have potential earnings on USD50,000s while having only committed USD1,000. Of course, potential earnings can also be potential losses and if your losses exceed the margin requirements, you must either replenish your broker account or allow the broker to close out your trade.

Figure 1.1 EUR/USD chart with trend lines

Trends

New traders often have difficulty in identifying the different trends that are taking place in the market. There are several patterns that you must learn to recognize which will help you decide when to place a trade. One of the most important points you must remember always is that "the trend is your friend" which essentially means never ever trade against the trend.

Knowing what the trend is, short term or long term, and knowing how strong the trend is are important for the trader to know. Currencies move in trends, either uptrends or downtrends, and there are also trends within trends. The EUR/USD monthly candlestick chart (Figure 1.1) shows three distinct trends as shown by the arrows. We have a downward trend from July 2011 to July 2012, followed by an upward trend from end of March 2013 to end of March 2014. Then from April 2014 to March 2015, we have another downward trend.

For now, do not worry about what a monthly candlestick chart means or shows, because in Chapter 2 we will be discussing this in detail. This is merely an introduction to help you understand what a trend is and how to identify it on a historical chart. Trends too will be dealt with a detail in chapters 2 and 3. In these chapters, we will discuss how we can recognize a developing short-term trend within a long-term trend. The chart above shows pictorially why you should treat the trend as your friend and not trade against its direction. If you do not follow the trend, you will lose.

Table 1.11 Currency pair correlations

Currency pair	Positive correlation	Negative correlation
EUR/USD	GBP/USD – AUD/USD NZD/USD	USD/CHF – USD/CAD
AUD/USD	NZD/USD – USD/JPN	USD/CHF – USD/CAD

Hedging

In the world of finance and investment, hedging is not an uncommon word. The term hedge fundamentally means that something is used to protect you against something that could hurt you. If we talk about hedging in the financial world, we can say that we use a hedge to protect our investments and assets against the risk of them losing value. A hedge is in effect a type of insurance that helps reduce financial risk. Therefore, the objective of a hedge is to reduce the potential risk as opposed to increasing the risk to try and earn some extra profit.

An investor in the currency market who sought to hedge a position would normally invest in two currency pairs that are negatively correlated. A negative correlation of two currency pairs is when one pair increases in value and the other pair usually decreases in value. By investing in negatively correlated products, the gains and the losses offset each other and the risk is minimized. More experienced traders use different types of hedging instruments such as forex swaps and forwards, interest rate swaps, futures, and options. We will look more closely at how to hedge and the characteristics of hedging instruments in later chapters (Table 1.11).

It makes sense that the higher the risk, the higher the opportunity, but also the greater can be the loss. As the risk is reduced by hedging, so is the potential for attaining the highest possible earnings. On the other hand, as the risk is reduced, then the potential for losing your investment is reduced as well.

Brokers

It is important that you fully understand your broker's privacy policy and not only why your broker needs the information he does but also what he intends to do with it. Brokers will always indicate in their policies that they will safeguard the personal and financial information of their clients and any guests to the website. They generally do not ask you if they can use your personal information. Mostly they imply that if you have opened an account with them or by using the broker's website you have consented to the collection and use of your personal information.

Most brokers generally require certain personal information such as name and address, email address, and telephone number to be able to get in touch with you. They will also need certain information which is required by law to see if you are who you say you are such as a social security number, a passport number, or tax identification number. Finally, the broker will collect information which they say helps in not only assessing your financial position including your net worth but also assess your previous trading experience if any. This information can include gender, birth date, occupation, and employment status. The regulatory bodies that regulate the online forex brokers will require that the broker has enough information to be able to assess available risk capital and net worth.

All this information is provided directly by completion of the necessary forms to open a demo or a real live trading account. Also, as you trade, or respond to a special offer, or send an email the broker can observe how you use the website and therefore provide additional services if needed.

MetaTrader 4 Trading Interface

Most brokers offer those who open a dummy or a live trading account two types of interface to facilitate trading. One is web based and each broker will provide an interface which will be similar in content but different in design. However, if you prefer to download and interface onto your laptop or desktop, most brokers will offer you the industry standard MetaTrader 4 (MT4) trading interface. This interface has now become the industry standard and provides you with all the information you will need to analyze the markets and make successful trades.

The MT4 displays live real-time exchange rates and other asset prices, charting tools, technical analysis tools, and fundamental analysis tools. It also keeps track of your trades in real time showing the current profit

Figure 1.2 MT4

or loss status of each trade as well as your overall position and profit or loss situation. Figure 1.2 shows the industry standard MT4 displaying a USD/CHF chart.

The main body of the MT4 is the chart, in this case a USD/CHF chart. Displayed along the top are the menus and various technical analysis functions. Down the left-hand side, the live prices for currencies and other assets are displayed. Across the bottom of the MT4 is information such as open and closed trades, profit or loss, fundamental analysis, and market news. The chart itself displays prices for the currency pair including current price as well as time periods displayed along the bottom of the chart. You will not be shown the mechanics of how to use the MT4 in this book because one of the reasons for opening a dummy account is not only to practice trading but also to become competent with the MT4 trading interface.

When Will I Be Ready?

Statistics show that 90 percent of traders lose money currency trading, 7 percent break even, and only 3 percent make money. So, if there is such a high rate of casualties, what are they not doing that they should be doing? The answer is that they are allowing emotions to get in the way of discipline and good money management. The solution to being a successful trader is being disciplined about the way you trade whatever the circumstances, even if you have made an awful trade. Make no mistake about it however; it is very hard to trade and at the same time keep your discipline. You must have a strategy that is comfortable for you. Do not look at the way other investors trade and follow them simply because they are making winning trades. Note how disciplined they are but be careful you might not be comfortable with the level of leverage they use or with the way they cover a losing trade.

You will need discipline to execute your trades through periods when you are not making any profit because you need to stay on course. When you are losing, it requires mental strength, confidence in your abilities and strategy, and above all discipline to stick with the strategy that served you well while you were winning. Make sure you are making informed trades, you have analyzed the fundamentals, understood the economic indicators, used the appropriate technical analysis, and above all that you are following your strategy, your trading plan.

Before even considering trading using a live account, it is crucial that you use a demo or dummy account extensively before you open a live online account and use it. The demo account gives you the opportunity to understand fully how the currency markets work as well as learn the basics of fundamental and technical analysis. Demo accounts mirror the live accounts in functionality and leverage. However, a demo account is not high risk as the money used is "play" money.

Once you move to a live account which is highly leveraged, unless you are disciplined, you could lose your whole investment very quickly. Be aware that any information such as opinion, research commentary, news which you find on websites that offer forex advice may not constitute smart or informed investment advice and therefore it is advisable not to trade high-risk funds on such opinion. No website, whether you are using their trading platform or not, will accept responsibility for your losses and your use of trading platforms, and trading high-risk funds on opinions from Internet sites is done completely at your own risk.

Always trade with money that you can afford to lose. Not with money that you have set aside to pay loans and household bills. Your trading judgment will always be objective if you trade money you can afford to be without. Learn to stand firm and do not take your profits too early. Holding on to profitable positions and riding the trends will maximize your gains. Keep your losses small by closing out a losing position immediately you realize you are wrong. Do not forget to place stop orders for all your trades as in this way you would not suffer heavy losses. Never overtrade, no matter how confident you are and no matter how long your winning streak is. It would not last and if you over extend yourself, the end of a winning streak could break you.

Discipline yourself to halve your capital outlay each time you add to a winning position. Do not make the mistake of doubling up, otherwise you will have a top-heavy pyramid that could come crashing down around you if the market turned against you. When things get tough and you are on a losing streak take a break and recharge yourself. Never put all your eggs in one basket. This could be disastrous. Split your capital into 10 equal parts and give yourself more opportunity for success.

It is also dangerous to add to a losing position by averaging. You cannot be certain up to what price the market will go against you. To average, you must double the capital used each time which is foolish. A good trader will cut his loss immediately. Be wise and remove profits from your trading account and put your winnings in a safe place. If you do not, the chances are good you will lose all your profits again. Prepare your game plan and stick to it. Decide what you are going to do when you are wrong and what you are going to do when you are right. Finally, decide on how much capital you are going to risk on every trade.

The transition from being a successful demo account trader to being a successful live account trader depends on your understanding yourself. It is easy to understand that you have the skills and the knowledge to trade successfully. It is not so easy to be able to say to yourself that you have conquered greed and that you do not make decisions from fear. However, once you can be truly honest with yourself, then you are ready to make the transition from demo to live account. There you have it. This chapter has given you enough information for you to choose a currency broker and open your first dummy account. Now, if you feel that you are ready, proceed to Chapter 2 and learn about key technical analysis tools, the forex charts.

CHAPTER 2

Candlestick Charts

In this chapter, we are going to discuss the types of price charts that are used by traders all over the world, both professional and retail. We shall mainly concentrate on candlestick charts as these specific charts are the most popular with traders today. By the time you have finished this chapter, you should have gained enough confidence to trade with some success on your dummy account using candlestick charts. Price chart's technical analysis is based on the premise that the current currency price is the culmination of everything that has happened in the past, and that historical and current chart patterns assist you to make correct trading decisions. When studying a price chart, you are in effect viewing price action patterns that have occurred in the past, and this should give you an awareness of where the price will be going in the future.

Price charts are calculated and presented in time periods and each point, line, or candle on the chart represents one time period. Table 2.1 gives the most common time periods used for both currency and stock price charts.

Table 2.1 *Time periods*

Time period
1 minute
5 minutes
15 minutes
30 minutes
1 hour
4 hours
1 day/daily
1 week
1 month

Charts Types

The most basic chart is the "line chart." The line chart consists of adjacent lines which connect all the closing prices of each time period together. Figure 2.1 shows a one-day period line chart for the USD/CHF currency pair.

As you can see from the line chart, it shows the level of currency closing prices but does not give you any other information. You can see how the price fluctuates over a period of time, as in this case, a series of daily periods covering several months. This is not a popular chart as it does not give you enough information to enable you to execute a successful strategy.

A second type of chart is the "bar chart," and this chart displays much more information than the line chart. It displays the closing and opening prices, plus the highest price and the lowest price of the day. This is the second most popular chart with traders who use a technical analysis approach to trading. The chart also displays time periods with each bar representing a specific time period (Figure 2.2).

The length of each bar shows the two extremes of the price action for the time period; the top of the bar shows the highest price and the bottom of the bar shows the lowest price. The left-hand side tag shows the opening price for that period and the right-hand tag shows the closing price. Notice how much more information there is on the bar chart compared with the line chart.

The most popular and most used chart of all is the candlestick chart. This chart has the same information as the bar chart, however it also gives

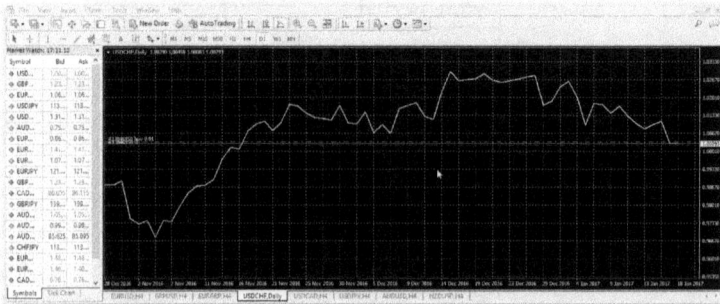

Figure 2.1 USD/CHF daily line chart

Figure 2.2 USD/CHF daily bar chart

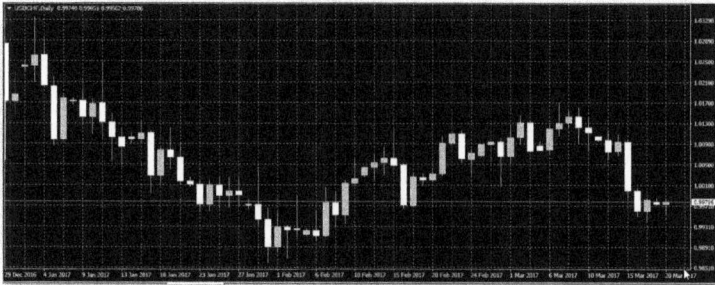

Figure 2.3 USD/CHF daily candlestick chart

information about the strength of the buyers and sellers. The candlesticks themselves have bodies and wicks as shown in the candlestick chart in Figure 2.3.

The white solid candles represent prices that are falling and the top of the body represents the opening price, the bottom of the body the closing price, and the extremes of the wicks the period high (top of the wick) and the period low price (bottom of the wick). The dark solid candles represent a rising price, the period high and low are represented by the wicks but the body now indicates the opening price at its bottom and the closing price at its top. Furthermore, the length of the top and bottom wicks (shadows) also gives an indication as to the strength of the buyers and sellers by their length above and below the body. A long upper shadow indicates an attempt by the buyers to take control but eventually lose out to the sellers. A long lower shadow indicates an attempt by the sellers to take control but eventually lose out to the buyers. Figures 2.4 and 2.5 show the components of a candlestick.

The term bull in trader's terminology means that the market is rising, therefore a bull candlestick is indicating, for a given time period, a rising currency pair. Similarly, the term bear means that the market is falling and the bear candlestick indicates a falling currency pair for a given time period.

Bull Candle

Upper Shadow/Wick ⟶

Period High

Closing Price ⟶

Main Body

Opening Price

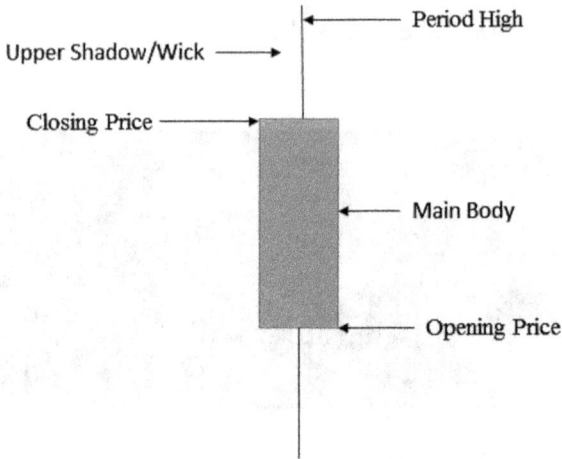

Figure 2.4 Bull candlestick

Bear Candle

Period High

Upper Shadow/Wick ⟶

Opening Price ⟶

Main Body

Closing Price

Lower Shadow/Wick ⟶

Period Low

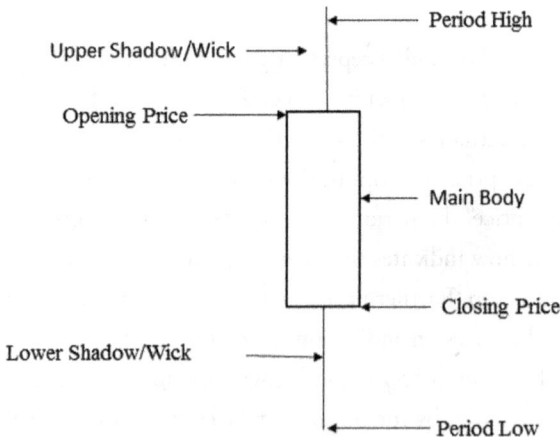

Figure 2.5 Bear candlestick

What Can the Single Candlestick Chart Tell You?

Candlestick charting first emerged in the 19th century in Japan where it was originally developed by a rice trader, hence its official name being Japanese candlestick chart. It was further developed and introduced to the West by Steve Nison in 1991. His many modifications and development of chart pattern interpretations led to candlestick charts becoming the popular trader's tool it is today.

The candlestick charts offer a more visually pleasing and therefore a simpler interpretation of currency price data than the traditional bar charts because a single candlestick gives a straightforward decipherable image of the price action. You are immediately able to compare the relationship between the high and low prices as well as the opening and closing prices. As you can see from Figure 2.6, there are several shapes to a single candlestick and each shape can give you vital information.

The white filled candlestick, which is marked "1," indicates a strong bearish trend during a 4-hour period with a lot of selling pressure. The candle has a full body, a small wick, and hardly a shadow below the main body. The candle opened at 1.0063 and closed at 1.0003, a fall of 60 pips in 4 hours.

The dark filled candle, which is marked "2," is the opposite of the previous candle and indicates a bullish trend with a lot of buying pressure. Again, this candle has very short wick and shadow. It opened at 1.0059 and closed at 1.0108, a rise of 49 pips in 4 hours.

The candle marked "3" opened at the beginning of the period at 0.9983 and fluctuated during the 4-hour period between a low of 0.9978 and a high of 1.0006 before closing at 0.9984, one pip higher than it

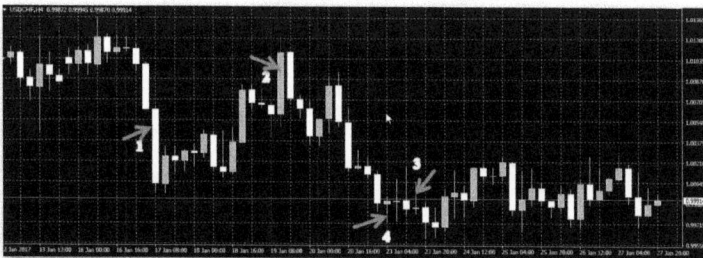

Figure 2.6 USD/CHF 4-hour candlestick chart

opened. This candle shows that the bulls were in charge for a while and there was buying pressure before the bears took over and selling pressure forced the price down again. This shape of candle with a long wick, very small body, and a short shadow indicates uncertainty in the market as to the direction of the currency pair. Any bullish or bearish partiality is based on the preceding and following price action.

The candle marked "4" shows that there was strong selling pressure during the 4-hour session, however buyers eventually came into the market and forced the price up toward the end of the session. This price action indicates market uncertainty with the opening and closing prices being only four pips apart and the lower shadow very long and the upper wick much shorter.

To identify exactly what the price action was during a session where the opening and closing prices are separated by a few pips, you must look at lower timeframes. For example, the left-hand candle in Figure 2.7 is a 1-hour candle and looking at it, there is no way that you could know the price movement during that 1-hour session. The price could, after opening, have moved up to the session high then fallen to the session low before moving up and closing a few pips above the opening.

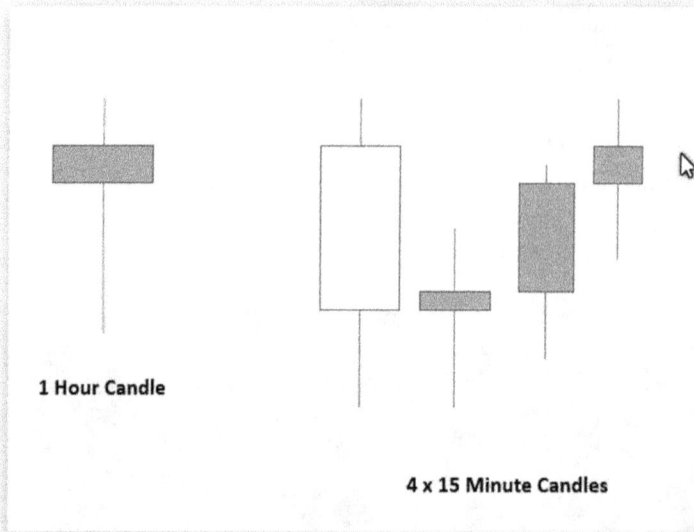

1 Hour Candle

4 x 15 Minute Candles

Figure 2.7 Price action analysis

However, if you change the chart to a 15-minute timeframe you can see the four 15-minute periods that make up the 1-hour session. Now the price action is clear. The session opened with a bearish sentiment and from the opening the price fell and the session and the 15-minute session ended with the price well down from the opening. In the next 15 minutes, there was a lot of indecision as the price fell even lower before recovering to just above the opening. In the subsequent 15-minute session after an initial fall, the bulls took over and push the price up further. Finally, in the final 15-minute session the price rose once more, again after an initial fall, before closing up in the session. Except for the first 15-minute candle, the next three showed some indecision in the market. This indecision is also reflected in the 1-hour candle too. Candles that represent indecision in the market are called doji. These are candles where the opening and closing prices are very close together with just a few pips difference. The USD/CHF daily chart in Figure 2.8 shows two types of doji candles.

One type is called spinning tops, which are doji candles that look like a spinning top and represents an indecision in the market which is not quite a balance between the bulls and the bears. The doji that shows complete balance between the bulls and the bears is the "indecision doji." Here the difference between the opening and closing prices is very small, just a few pips. This doji type can also occur where there is low volume in the market and no momentum to move the price very much.

As you can see, a candlestick chart is a technical analysis tool where each candle indicates a specific price action, however, on its own it does

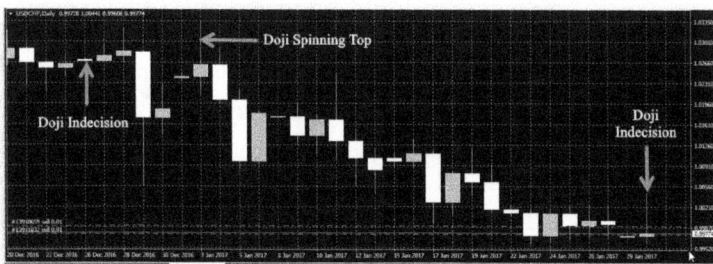

Figure 2.8 USD/CHF daily chart showing doji candles

not suggest the future direction of the currency pair. In the next section, we will start to interpret the most common types of candlestick patterns that are the most important for you to trade successfully.

Interpreting Chart Patterns

The basic tenets behind technical analysis are that price action trends, and history always repeats itself. A chart pattern which shows an uptrend indicates that the bulls (buyers) are in control and the currency is in demand. When the chart pattern shows a downtrend, it shows that the sellers (bears) are in control and the currency is over supplied. The price action, however, does not move in the same direction forever and the balance between buyers and sellers is constantly changing. It is at these points that chart patterns emerge showing us that there is a likelihood of a change. These changes could be long- or short term, precipitated by market sentiment where published economic data are worse or better than expected or investors seeking to invest in a perceived strong currency or sell out of a perceived weakening currency. Or, where the market in a specific currency pair has become overbought or oversold in the short term and the price is set to retrace. An asset being overbought is when an almost continuous upward trend in the price of an asset that depletes all the buyers for the asset. Then the asset becomes exposed to a price reversal because all those who sought to buy it most likely have it, therefore supply forces start to outweigh demand forces, leading to selling pressure on the asset. An oversold position is exactly the opposite, where continuous selling exhausts the number of sellers of an asset and demand forces start to outweigh supply forces, leading to buying pressure on the asset.

There are many candle patterns that signpost the probable price action in the near or far future and we shall be discussing these later in this chapter. However, one such pattern shows a very strong trend, as shown in Figure 2.9, where the price action moves between support and resistance levels.

The chart in Figure 2.9 displays a lot of information about the price action over several months for the USD/CHF currency pair. The key

Figure 2.9 USD/CHF daily chart support and resistance

price action movements have been numbered to enable you to identify what they are.

1. This arrow points to a white line at the price level 0.9960 which forms a support line and shows that in September and November the USD/CHF price could not break through below this level.

2. This arrow points to a white line at price level 0.9860 which forms a support line and shows that in early October 2016 and January 2017 the price could not break through this level, although in late October 2016 the bears managed to break through the support level.

3. This arrow points to a white line at price level 0.9951 which forms a resistance line. In mid-October 2016, the bulls for several days were trying to push the price above 0.9951 but were unsuccessful and the USD/CHF price plummeted soon after.

4. This arrow points to a white line at price 1.0300 which forms a resistance line and shows that in December 2016 the USD/CHF price could not break through this resistance level and eventually the price fell at the end of the year.

5. This arrow points to the white line at price level 0.9951 which formed a resistance level in October 2016 but in mid-January 2017 formed a support level. This line shows that resistance levels can become support levels and vice versa.

6. These two arrows point to trend channels where on the left channel the price rose almost continuously for a month and on the

right-hand channel the price fell almost continuously for a month. Notice that the top line of the channels follows a line of resistance, while the bottom line of the channels follows a line of support. There was another strong upward trend during November 2016 but drawing more channel lines would have made the chart too jumbled for you.

Head and Shoulders Reversal Pattern

Candlestick patterns fall into two distinct types: reversal and continuation patterns. A reversal pattern is when the candle pattern signals a probable reversal of the current trend, while the continuation pattern signals a continuation of the current trend. One of the most easily identifiable candle reversal patterns is shown in Figure 2.10. It is called the head and shoulders reversal pattern.

This pattern signals that a possible change in the current trend is going to happen. Its shape is like the head and shoulders of a person. The left-hand bullish candles form the left shoulder, while the next four candles form the head, and the right-hand bearish white candles form the right shoulder. The price action shows a rise of 51 pips on the left shoulder before a reversal in trend on the right shoulder shows a decline in price of 46 pips. The head and shoulders pattern only appears when an upward trend loses its momentum and a trend reversal is imminent.

Figure 2.10 Head and shoulders reversal pattern

Triple Candlestick Patterns

As the description suggests, triple candlestick patterns are patterns made up of three candles. These patterns can either be in continuation or reversal patterns.

Bearish Continuation Pattern—Falling Three Method

The falling three method is a bearish continuation pattern where a bearish trend takes a short break before continuing in its original direction. Figure 2.11 shows what the pattern looks like.

The falling three method begins with a long white bearish candle followed by a series of upward bullish candles. These candles all form within the range of the original candle, but have smaller bodies. The fifth and final candle is the same as the original trend candle but it closes at a new low. The market has been in a downtrend. A long white candle forms, followed by a series of smaller candles, each consecutively

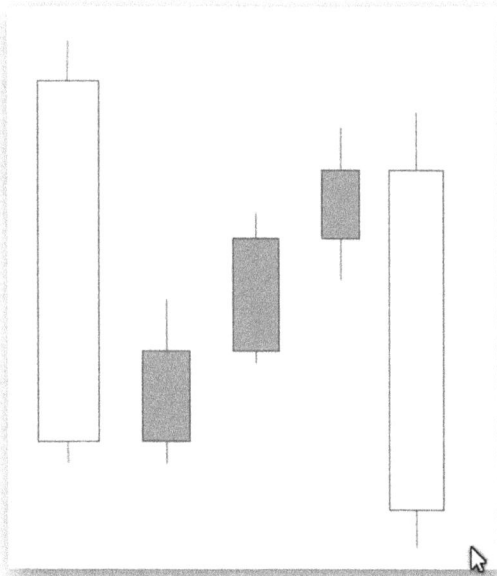

Figure 2.11 Falling three method

getting higher. The optimal number of up trending days should be three. However, two, four, or five counter trend days can be observed. The important factors are that they do not close *above* the open of the big white candles and that the shadows do not go above the white candle's open. The final day of the formation should close lower than the first big white candle's close.

Bullish Continuation Pattern—Rising Three Method

The rising three method is the opposite of the falling three method and is a bullish continuation pattern. Figure 2.12 shows what the optimal pattern looks like.

The rising three method begins with a long bullish candle followed by a series of downward bearish candles. These candles all form within the range of the original candle, but have smaller bodies. The fifth and final candle is the same as the original trend candle but it closes at a new high. The market has been in an uptrend. A long

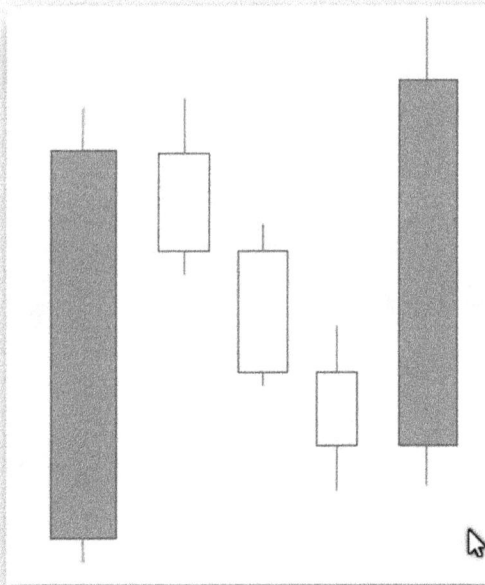

Figure 2.12 Rising three method

bullish candle forms, followed by a series of small candles, each consecutively getting lower. The optimal number of down trending days should be three. However, two, four, or five counter trend days can be observed. The important factors are that they do not close below the open of the big candle and that the shadows do not go below the candle's open. The final day of the formation should close higher than the first candle's close.

Three Inside Up Candle Pattern

The three inside up candlestick construction is a trend-reversal pattern that is found at the lower most point of a downtrend. This triple candlestick pattern indicates that the downtrend is probably over and a new uptrend has started. Figure 2.13 shows what a typical three inside up candle pattern looks like.

The properties of this candlestick formation are that the first candle should be found at the bottom of a downtrend and characterized by a long bearish candlestick. The second candle should close at or above the midpoint of the first candle. The third candlestick needs to close above the first candle's high to confirm that buyers have overpowered the seller's momentum and the downtrend has ended.

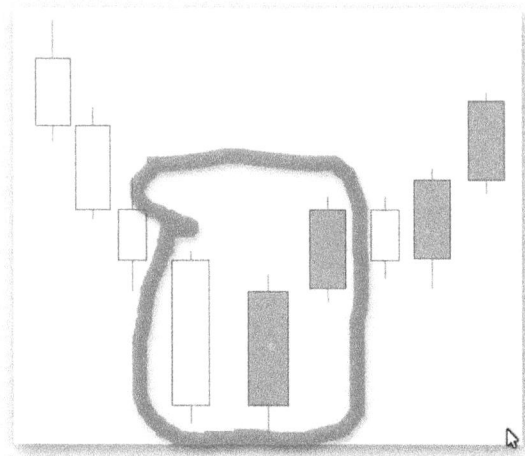

Figure 2.13 Three inside up candle pattern

Three Inside Down Candle Pattern

The three inside down candlestick construction is also a trend-reversal pattern but is the opposite of the three inside up pattern. It is found at the highest most point of an uptrend. This triple candlestick pattern indicates that the uptrend is probably over and a new downtrend has started. Figure 2.14 shows what a typical three inside down candle pattern looks like.

The properties of this candlestick formation are that the first candle of the pattern is found at the top of an uptrend and characterized by a long bullish candle. The second candle should close at or below the midpoint of the first candle. The third candlestick needs to close below the first candle's low to confirm that sellers have overpowered the buyer's momentum and the uptrend has ended.

Morning Star

The morning star is a triple candlestick pattern that is usually formed at the end of a downtrend. It is a reversal pattern that can be recognized through these characteristics. Figure 2.15 shows what a typical morning star pattern looks like.

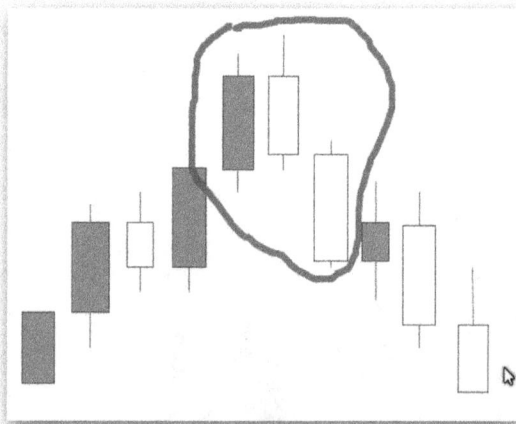

Figure 2.14 Three inside down candle pattern

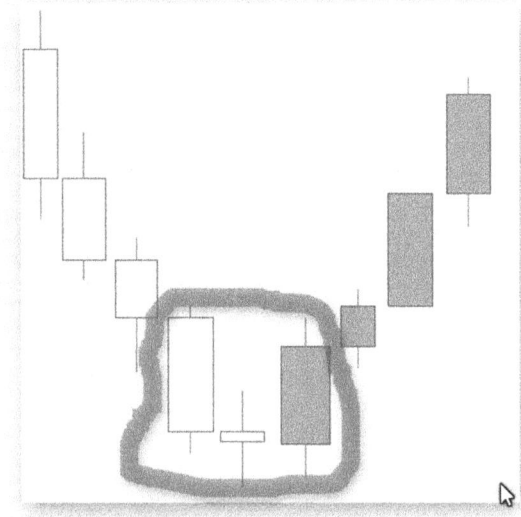

Figure 2.15 Morning star candle pattern

The first candlestick is a bearish candle, which is the final candle of a recent downtrend. The second candle has a small body, indicating that there could be some indecision in the market. This candle can be either bullish or bearish. The third candle acts as a confirmation that a reversal is in place, as the candle closes beyond the midpoint of the first candle.

Evening Star

The evening star is a triple candlestick pattern that is usually formed at the end of an uptrend. It is a reversal pattern that can be recognized through these characteristics. Figure 2.16 shows what a typical evening star pattern looks like.

The first candlestick is a bullish candle, which is the final candle of a recent uptrend. The second candle has a small body, indicating that there could be some indecision in the market. This candle can be either bullish or bearish. The third candle acts as a confirmation that a reversal is in place, as the candle closes beyond the midpoint of the first candle.

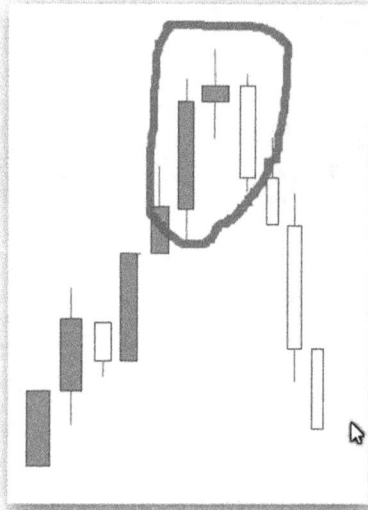

Figure 2.16 Evening star candle pattern

Dual Candlestick Patterns

As the name suggests dual candlestick patterns are formed by two candles that are next to each other. All dual candlestick patterns indicate a possible reversal of the current trend.

Tweezer Tops and Bottoms

The tweezers are dual candlestick reversal patterns and are typically spotted after an extended uptrend or downtrend, signifying that a possible reversal will occur soon. Figure 2.17 shows that a typical tweezers formation looks like a pair of tweezers.

The *tweezer candlestick patterns* have the following characteristics. The first candlestick is in the same direction as the overall trend. If prices are moving up, then the first candle should be bullish. The second candlestick is against the overall trend, so if prices are moving up, then the second candle should be bearish. The shadows of the candlesticks should be of equal length and tweezer tops should have the same highs, while tweezer bottoms should have the same lows. If prices are moving down, then the first candle is bearish and the second bullish.

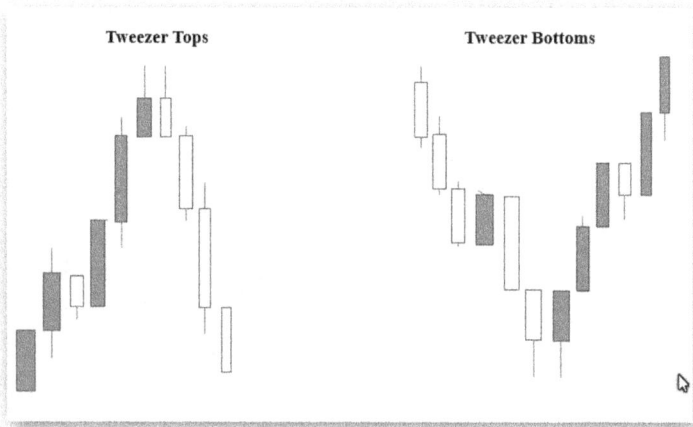

Figure 2.17 Tweezers candlestick pattern

Engulfing Candles

There are two engulfing candle patterns. Figure 2.18 shows the bearish engulfing and the bullish engulfing patterns.

The *bearish engulfing pattern* occurs when the bullish candle is immediately followed by a bearish candle that completely "engulfs" it. This means that sellers overpowered the buyers and that a strong move downward could happen. The *bullish engulfing pattern* is the opposite of the bearish engulfing pattern in that it signals a strong upward move may be coming. It happens when a bearish candle is immediately followed by a larger bullish candle. This second candle "engulfs" the bearish candle. This means buyers are flexing their muscles and that there could be a strong upward move after a recent downtrend or a period of consolidation.

Single Candlestick Patterns

Single candlestick patterns are formed as an indication that the market is at a potential point of reversal.

Hammer and Hanging Man

Although the hammer and hanging man look identical they have totally different meanings which is conditional on previous price action.

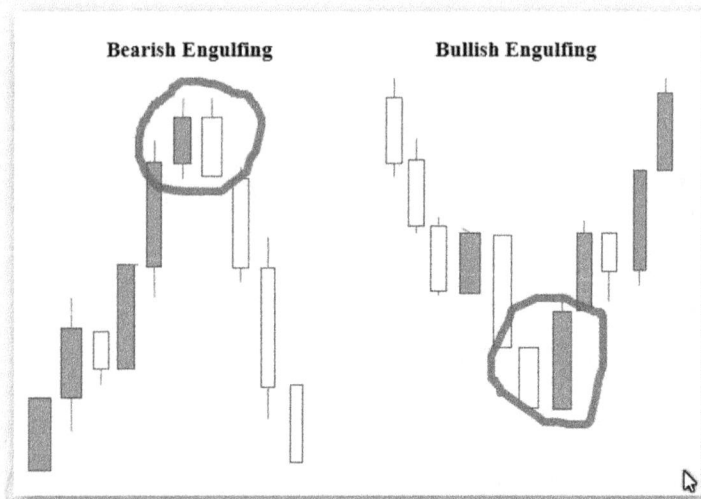

Figure 2.18 Engulfing candle patterns

As shown in Figure 2.19, both have little bodies (bullish or bearish), long lower shadows, absent upper shadows, or very small upper shadows.

The *hammer* (see Figure 2.20) is a reversal pattern that forms during a downtrend. When prices are falling, hammer-shaped candlesticks are bullish signals that indicate that potentially the bottom of a trend is near and that prices will start rising again. The long lower shadow indicates that sellers pushed prices lower, but buyers managed to overcome this selling pressure and the price closed near the open.

Caution, just because you see a hammer form in a downtrend does not mean you automatically place a buy order! More bullish confirmation is needed before it is safe to pull the trigger. We shall discuss more fully how we can confirm buy and sell signals in later chapters; however, for now a possible confirmation would be to wait for a bullish candlestick to close above the open to the right side of the hammer.

The following criteria determines a hammer candlestick.

- The long shadow is three or more times the length of the real body.
- Tiny or no upper shadow.
- The real body is at the upper end of the trading range.
- The body can be bullish or bearish.

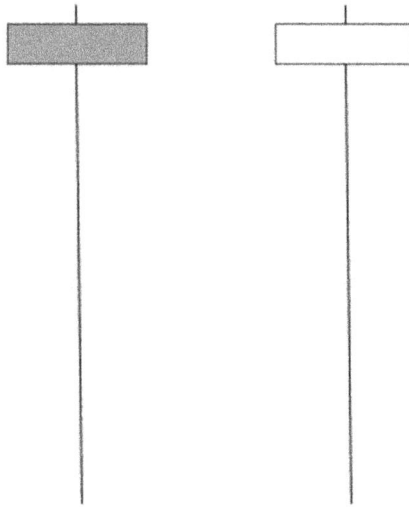

Figure 2.19 Hammer and hanging man candles

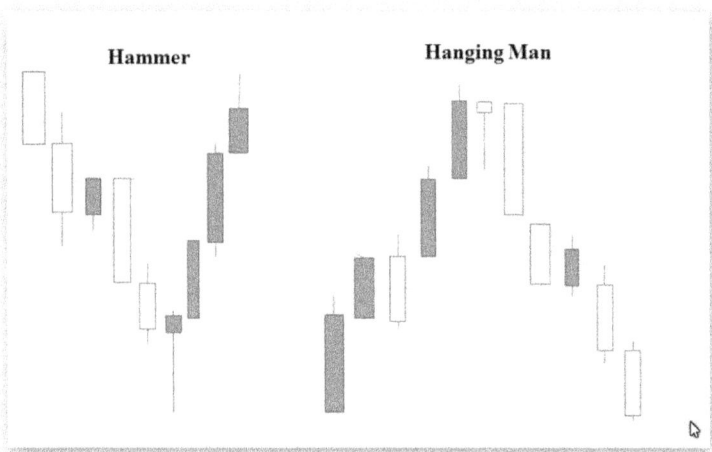

Figure 2.20 Hammer and hanging man candle patterns

The *hanging man* (see Figure 2.20) is a reversal pattern that forms during an uptrend which can also indicate a price top or a strong resistance level. When prices are rising, the development of a hanging man indicates that sellers are beginning to outnumber buyers. The long lower shadow demonstrates that sellers pushed prices lower during the session. Buyers struggled to push the price back up and could only manage to push it to near the opening. This potentially indicates that there are few buyers left to be able to provide enough momentum to keep the prices rising.

The criteria that determines a hanging man candlestick is like the hammer candle except that the color matters more and a white or bearish body is more bearish than a dark bullish body.

Inverted Hammer and Shooting Star

The inverted hammer and shooting star also look identical. The only difference between them is whether you are in a downtrend or uptrend. Both candlesticks have small bodies (bullish or bearish), long upper shadows, and tiny or no lower shadows as shown in Figure 2.21.

The *inverted hammer* happens when prices have been falling and it is a bullish pattern that indicates the possibility of a reversal. The hammer's long upper shadow shows that buyers have tried to push the price higher. Sellers realizing what the buyers were doing attempted to push the price back down again. However, the buyers still managed to close the session near the opening price. The fact that sellers were not able to push the

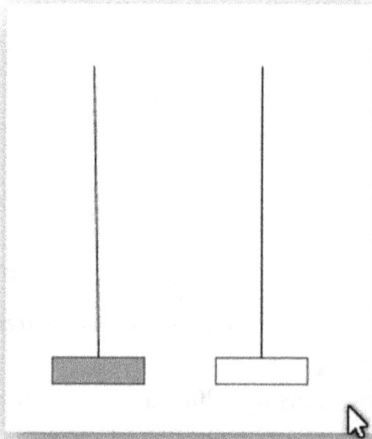

Figure 2.21 Inverted hammer and shooting star candles

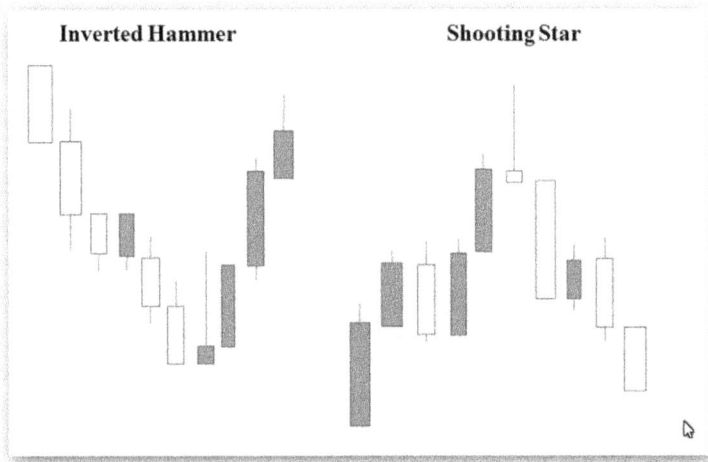

Figure 2.22 Inverted hammer and shooting star candle pattern

price any lower is a good indication that all those wanting to sell have already sold. That just leaves buyers in the market.

The *shooting star* is a bearish reversal pattern that looks indistinguishable to the inverted hammer and happens when prices have been rising. Its shape indicates that the price action opened at its low and then rallied, but then pulled back to the bottom at the end of the session. This indicates that buyers tried to push the price up, but the sellers came in and overwhelmed them. This is a certain bearish sign, since there are no more buyers left, only sellers (Figure 2.22).

On both the inverted hammer and the shooting star it does not matter whether the body of the candle is bullish or bearish.

The candlestick patterns you have been shown in this chapter are the most popular patterns used by professional traders today. Once you have mastered these and learnt to recognize them, you will trade with more confidence that the patterns displayed on your candlestick charts are giving you clear trade signals. In the following chapters, we will study other technical analysis tools that you can utilize to confirm the trade signals displayed on your charts are good signals.

CHAPTER 3

Technical Analysis

In this chapter, we will discuss the kinds of technical analysis indicators and tools used by forex, stock, and commodity traders all over the globe. We will concentrate on the indicators that are most popular with professional and retail traders alike. By the end of this chapter, you will have gained enough confidence to start trading with success on a live account using your own capital.

All the technical indicators that we will discuss in this book are available on the universal MT4 trading platform by clicking on the "Insert" tab on the main menu and then choosing the menu item "Indicators" in the dropdown menu.

Like many novice forex traders, you will have little success and a lot of losses at the beginning. However, do not give up, forex trading is not something you can rush into without an education. Take your time to learn the ropes. Also, get yourself a mentor, someone you trust who is a professional trader preferably and can give you measured advice. Self-educate yourself by reading books while trading on your dummy account. What are the important things to learn? First and foremost, it is charting and technical analysis. We have covered charting at length in the last chapter, so in this chapter we will discuss the most popular technical analysis tools used by traders today.

Importance of Technical Analysis

To make any kind of money in the forex market, you should focus on the technical analysis indicators to understand what they are telling you. At first, use the most common indicators, then once you have mastered these, you can go onto master some of the more complex ones. The most common technical analysis tools that professional and retail traders use are classed as trend indicators. In this chapter, we shall be discussing these as well as the indicators classed as oscillators.

Why do traders use technical analysis? The answer to that question is quite simple, it works! The reality is that there are thousands of traders who repeatedly make money in the markets who use technical analysis as their prime tool. It is not that technical analysis is the holy grail or that it is a so-called voodoo science. Technical analysis is math and statistical based. It looks at the historic performance of currencies and uses modern technology to analyze the future behavior of prices.

It is believed to be more accurate than fundamental analysis (we will discuss fundamental analysis in Chapter 4) because it is supported by cold, hard facts, but in the end, there is no 100 percent fail safe way to foretell the currency market's actions. Technical analysts input past price information into a computer which then supplies data on the patterns that have taken place in over a century of forex trading. These patterns are evaluated with real-time price movements and forecasts are made.

Another rationale behind the fact that most forex traders utilize technical analysis is because it is factual and easy to follow. It offers facts and statistics, not just data that can be interpreted in any way you want. That means it allows you to benefit from the consistency in the data you use and enables an even playing field. With the arrival of young professionals like you into the dominion of forex trading, it is not hard to comprehend why technology is involved. Brought up on a staple diet of computers and technology, instant fulfillment and easy acquirement of knowledge, the computer-age group has engaged technical analysis with delight.

One of the reasons that technical analysis is a powerful tool is that it is flexible and can be used by traders in different disciplines. Traders trading one currency pair can easily switch to another currency pair and be just as successful by applying the same knowhow. A trader who switches to trading other assets such as commodities or stocks can successfully apply the same techniques.

There are skeptics who say that the charts only reflect what the trader wants them to reflect and in fact everything is random, so if past patterns were random so future patterns will be random also. However, the question that needs an answer is "can the study of past action help us predict the future more accurately?" The emphatic answer is "yes." Just think about how the weather is forecast. Huge computers are employed to look at the patterns of the weather over the last hundred years and then predict what the weather will be like tomorrow. It works because weather systems, markets, economies, and industry are constantly repeating themselves. Everything is cyclical. Charts are almost an art form and even though they are scientifically created, they can also be esthetic and colorful to behold, so the trader needs only to analyze and interpret them. The trained eye of a trader proves time and time again that technical analysis works and that is why most traders use it. As a new trader, you should try to master interpreting the information each chart conveys and use the information as your partner in helping you make profitable trades.

The indicators you will be learning about in this chapter should not be used in isolation but used together with charts, fundamental analysis, and at least one other indicator as confirmation of an entry price for a trade. In this way, your trading will not be gambling but it will be based on factual data and analysis that gives you the advantage over pure luck.

Trends and Trend Lines

A trend is a price movement in a specific direction either up, down, or sideways which lasts for a length of time. In an uptrend, prices show higher highs and higher lows than previous sessions, while in a downtrend, prices have lower highs and lower lows than the previous session.

A trend will help you identify where the price action is going and therefore enable you to enter a trade early in the trend and confidently stay with it until it peaks or until it bottoms out. It keeps us from staying too long with a position where we might lose some of our gains. The use of trend lines allows us to identify the peaks and thereby exit the trade at the highest point or identify the lows so that we can buy at the lowest point possible. The converse is true if you are looking at trading a downward trend. Essentially the markets move up, move down, or move sideways, so there are only three types of trends to study.

Figure 3.1 shows several trends throughout the 11 years spanning the AUD/USD monthly chart. I have identified four of them for you, however I am sure you will be able to identify the other trends on the

Figure 3.1 AUD/USD monthly chart – trend lines

chart. The trend marked (1) is a strong upward trend lasting from April 2006 to early July 2008. The trend marked (2) is a strong downtrend which began in September 2014 and finished in September 2015. The trends that have been marked (3) and (4) are ranging trends where the price stays between an upper range (top horizontal line) and a lower range (bottom horizontal line). Notice how the ranges which are at each end of the 11-year span have the same upper price resistance level (0.7694) and the same lower price support level (0.7166). In the next section, we shall discuss support and resistance levels in more detail and look at some of the rules which you as a trader should take on board to successfully trade these levels.

Let us look at the trend marked (1) again. It is an upward trend and the trend line is drawn along the price bottoms ensuring that at least two bottoms are touching the line. Most or all the bottoms are higher than the bottom immediately before them. This line serves as a line of support and when eventually that support line is broken, as you can see from the chart, the trend has reversed.

When there is a downtrend, as marked by (2), notice that the trend line is drawn joining the tops with at least two tops touching the line. Also, all the tops are lower than the top immediately preceding them. When the trend bottoms out, you will notice the last top has risen above the top immediately before it. This signaled a change in the trend and the start of not an uptrend but a ranging trend marked by (4) on the chart.

Most traders would not trade trend lines on a monthly chart, they would use the chart as a confirmation that a trend is in progress. However,

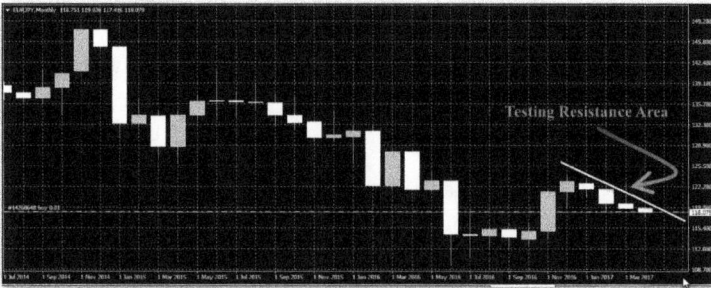

Figure 3.2 EUR/JPY monthly chart

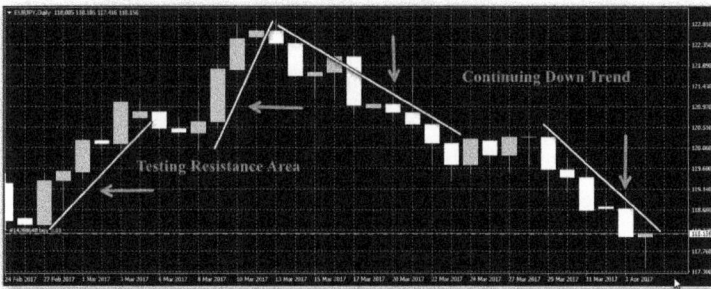

Figure 3.3 EUR/JPY daily chart

they would trade trend lines on a daily chart or a lower timeframe such as 4-hour or 1-hour chart. If we look at the EUR/JPY monthly chart from January 1, 2017, to April 4, 2017, and draw a trend line, we see that there has been a downtrend for the first few months of the year (Figure 3.2).

In March, the market tested the resistance line when the bulls broke through for a while, (the upper wick is through the trend line), before the bears pushed the price down again. Now if we drill down and look at a daily chart for March 2017 we can see this price action on the chart (Figure 3.3).

In the chart, we can see two mini-uptrends from February 27 through March 10, which test the resistance area of our trend line on the monthly chart. The bears eventually resist the bulls and the long-term downtrend continues through early April 2017. It is important to remember that trend lines indicate areas of support and resistance levels and are not exact numbers. You will often see prices move through a support or resistance level before retracing back to the trend line.

Trading Trend Lines

Price charts can produce many price moves and random movements that are called "noise" and can cause you to find it difficult to identify a new trend as it forms. Therefore, when starting out as a new trader, you should draw as many trend lines as possible in every direction on your chart, where there are two highs or two lows that can be connected. Particularly on the right-hand side of the chart, where the most recent price action is located. Now you can analyze the chart using the chart reading abilities you learnt in Chapter 2 together with what you have learnt about trend lines. You can see the pullbacks and the short-term trends from the long-term trends (see Figure 3.4).

There are many trend lines drawn on this chart varying from 2-day trends to 2-week trends. A trend line is usually redrawn many times as the trend runs its course and on the chart the original trend line drawn at the beginning of the upward trend on the left side of the chart is steep, while a final redrawn trend line shown is much less steep and more accurate. Do not be afraid of continually redrawing your trend lines as the trend continues, as this will give you a more accurate picture of what price action is about to happen and you can react accordingly. Also, shown on the chart is a ranging trend denoted by the two parallel lines. Here, the price action fluctuates between an upper price range and a lower price range before breaking through the resistance at the start of a new uptrend.

Figure 3.4 USD/CAD daily price chart

On the chart, you can see that the steeper the trend line is, the more likely it will be broken by a pull-back. This does not necessarily mean that a reversal is in progress but more likely that the price action was too strong to be sustained and the action reverted to a more moderate pace.

All trading software including the MT4 trading platform and other charting platforms should have a trendline or line tool. Choose the tool, then for an uptrend, connect the line from the low of one candle to the low of the next, and then extend it out to the right to provide a projection of where the next candle lows might occur. For a downtrend, connect the high of one candle to the high of the next candle and then extend it out to the right. The lines provide a projection for where future candle highs might occur.

Once you have drawn your trend lines you need to decide if the trend will continue or there will be a reversal or a pull-back and then a continuation of the current trend. To make the decision you will also have to use your charting skills and read what the candles are telling you. However, armed with your charting skills and accurate trend lines, it would be too risky to decide on an entry strategy at this point. You should always use a third indicator to confirm your decision before entering a trade. We will discuss the indicators you can use to confirm your trade entry point during the rest of this chapter.

Moving Averages

Traders are continually on the lookout for an indicator that tells them the optimum moment to buy or sell a currency. A popular tool that you can use, to not only spot market noise (small fluctuations in a market trend) and avoid trading it, is the moving average. Moving averages are fundamentally a set of data points which in the case of an asset's price is a chosen number of closing prices during a specific time period which are joined together by a line drawn on a candlestick price chart. The time periods most commonly used are 1 minute, 5 minutes, 15 minutes, 30 minutes, 60 minutes, 4 hours, daily, weekly, or monthly. The most common number of moving average series of closing prices used is 5, 10, 20, 50, 100, and 200. There are three commonly used moving average types used by traders today.

Simple Moving Average

The simple moving average (SMA) is calculated by adding the number of closing prices for the number of periods chosen and then dividing the total by the number of periods. For example, if we had a 10-period moving average on a 60-minute timeframe, the closing prices for the last 10 hours are added together and then divided by 10. The result would become the latest data point and the furthest data point or closing price would be dropped.

Exponential Moving Average

The exponential moving average (EMA) differs from the SMA in that it does not drop the first price in a series when the latest price is calculated. If, for example, we have specified a 10 series EMA, the first calculation will be the same as the SMA, however when the next price in the series becomes available the calculation will retain the original 10 prices plus the new price to arrive at the new average. The EMA line consequently follows the price action much more closely than the SMA.

Linearly Weighted Moving Average

This moving average is calculated in the same manner as the SMA but uses averages that are linearly weighted to ensure that the most recent prices have the greatest impact on the average. This is done by giving the oldest price in the calculation the weight of one, with the next oldest the weight of two, and the next one three all the way up to the latest price which has the highest weighting. Figure 3.5 shows a EUR/USD 60-minute chart where all three forms of moving averages of 20 periods have been drawn.

The SMA is the smoother of the three lines and the linear weighted moving average is the choppier of the three. The EMA follows the price action more closely than the SMA. Both the EMA and more so, the linear moving average, signal a trend change much sooner than the SMA does. However, this could cause a trader to enter a trade too soon and find that the price action was just a small pull-back and that the initial direction of the trend continued. This is the main reason that most traders prefer to use the SMA.

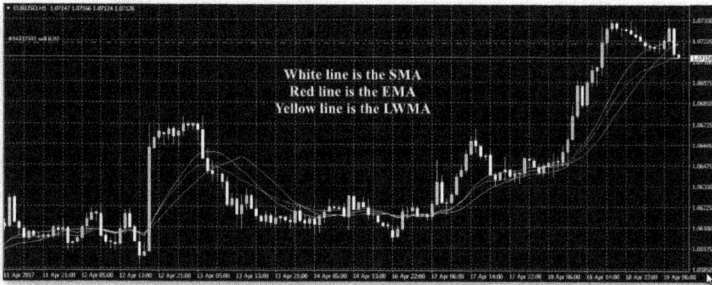

Figure 3.5 EUR/USD 1-hour chart

Moving Average Crossovers

Moving averages are used to identify, as well as confirm, price trends and identify support and resistance levels. If the price action is above a 20-period SMA it is an indication of a bullish trend, if it is below the moving average it indicates a bearish trend. However, what a single moving average line cannot show you is trade exit and entry points. To use moving averages to signal a trade entry or a trade exit, you will need to use three moving averages on one price chart.

Let us go back to our EUR/USD price chart and again draw three SMA lines but this time use different periods. We will use a 5-period, a 10-period, and a 20- period SMA on a 1-hour price chart (see Figure 3.6).

The white line is the 5-period moving average. This line is termed the fast line as it is much more sensitive to the price action than the other lines. The 10-period moving average line, moves with a smoother action and is less responsive to price action than the 5-period moving average. The 20-period moving average is an even smoother line than the 10 period line. Of course, you could use any number of time periods for your moving average, however, most traders use the time periods I have explained so far and therefore if you use the same time periods the trends are more likely to be real and not fake because thousands of other traders are seeing the same as you.

You can use the crossover point where the white line (5-period moving average) crosses up over or down under the 10-period moving average as a trade signal to buy when the line crosses up or to sell when the line crosses down. If the white line crosses the 20-period moving average, it

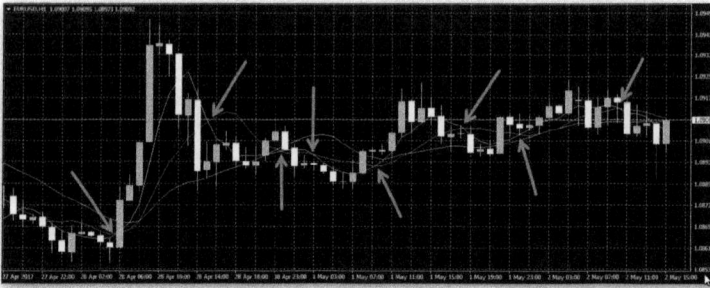

Figure 3.6 EUR/USD 1-hour chart—three moving averages

Table 3.1 Pip gains on six moving average crossovers on EUR/USD hourly chart

Trend	Open rate	Close rate	Pips gained
Up	1.0866	1.0908	42
Down	1.0908	1.0897	11
Down	1.0897	1.0892	5
Up	1.0892	1.0906	14
Down	1.0906	1.0903	3
Up	1.0903	1.0913	10

is an indication of the start of a strong trend. In Figure 3.6 the arrows indicate where the crossovers are. If you had traded on each of those trade signals you would have made 85 pips. Table 3.1 shows how you could have traded the crossovers to make the 85 pips.

Suppose each trade was for EUR1,000,000, then the total profit for the six trades would have been EUR8,500. Redundant crossovers can also act as points of resistance and support. As you can see from Figure 3.7 when a 50-period and a 100-period moving average is added to the chart and we change the chart to a weekly timeframe, both these moving averages, as indicated by the arrows, act as support or resistance lines.

Trading the moving average crossover is a favorite trading strategy for many traders because this indicator is what is called a lagging indicator, which means it eliminates market noise, rendering the buy or sell signals more accurate. We can see this in Figure 3.8 which is a EUR/USD daily chart.

Figure 3.7 EUR/USD weekly chart

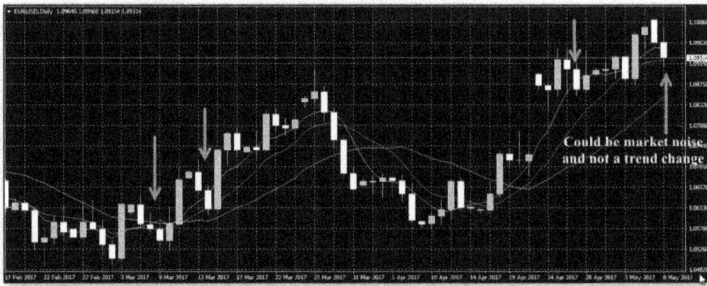

Figure 3.8 EUR/USD daily chart

I have marked on the chart areas where, without the hindsight of being able to look back at the price action, you might have believed that the current trend had ended and a new trend began. Simply drawing a trend line might lead you to believe this, however by using a moving average crossover you would wait until the fast line (5-period moving average) had crossed the slower line (10-period moving average) before you made your trading decision. The areas indicated by the arrows were in fact market noise and the trend continued. The far-right bear candles look as though a bearish trend is developing, however until the white moving average line crosses down through the 10-period moving average line, you should stay in the trade.

Moving Average Cross-Trading Strategy—Trading Plan

As we have seen, the moving average cross is a simple system that is easy to follow, uses simple indicators, and because moving averages lag, they avoid us trading market noise. Before we make a trade using this system, I want to tell you about trading plans. Every trader should have a trading plan because a good plan takes out the emotional and indecision aspect of trading and allows the trader to trade in a business-like manner. The plan should incorporate conditions for entering a trade, stop-loss triggers, take-profit triggers, the setting for the trailing stop, and the conditions for exiting a trade.

A *stop-loss order* is the price at which if you are in a losing trade you trigger an exit from the trade. Always use a stop loss to prevent any big losses on trades. The number of pips difference between your entry price and stop-loss price will depend on what technical analysis system you are using.

The *take-profit order* is the price or profit level at which you want to be exited from the trade at a profit. Usually the number of pips difference between the entry price and the take-profit price is a multiple of the number of pips in the stop loss. I generally recommend a setting that is twice the number of stop-loss pips. The take-profit price represents your exit strategy and stops you being too greedy. Many traders make the mistake of seeing the price approach their take-profit price and believing that they can make more gains, they reset or disable the take profit and then find that the market reverses and they gain less profit or even get into a losing trade situation.

The *trailing stop order* is a stop loss that is set at a specified number of pips in front of the entry price. For example, if the trailing stop is set at 10 pips forward from the entry price, once the price has been reached, the stop moves forward with the price action. However, if the price action reverses once it has reversed 10 pips, the trade is automatically exited, thereby preventing a losing trade. I recommend a trailing stop order set at 25 percent of the take-profit order.

Trade exit conditions are either hitting the take-profit trigger or hitting the stop-loss trigger.

If you keep rigidly to a trading plan that uses stop-loss and take-profit orders you would not find yourself making emotional decisions or going through periods of indecision and big losses.

Now let us get back to our moving average strategy.

First, although we could use any timeframe and currency pair, for this strategy setup we are going to use our hourly EUR/USD chart. It is interesting to note that professional traders in major global banks tend to use the moving average cross together with support and resistance areas as their principle trading indicators, simply because they are simple and easily set up. In our strategy, we will use the 5-, 10-, and 20-period moving average. Our entry condition is to enter a long trade when our fast-moving average (5-period FMA) crosses the slower moving average (10-period SMA) from below, or, enter a short trade when the FMA crosses the SMA from above. In our setup, we are going to make a short trade where the FMA crosses the SMA from above as indicated in Figure 3.9.

The FMA crossed the SMA at the price 1.0970. At this point, we would enter a sell trade. At the same time, we would set our stop-loss order at the high of the candle immediately before the cross, (for a buy trade, the stop loss is set at the low of the candle immediately before the cross). Our stop loss is at the 1.0984 price level. This ensures that if the trade turns sour, we will only lose 14 pips. I use a reward risk ratio of 1:2, so I generally set my take-profit order at twice the amount of my stop-loss pips. So, the take-profit pips should be 28 pips at the price of 1.0942. As you can see from the chart, the price falls to 1.0927 before the FMA crosses above the SMA to end the downward trend. If we had not set a take-profit trigger, we could have made an extra 15 pips but that would have been a little greedy and violated our trading plan.

As we can see from this example of a potential trade, the moving average crossover is a technical analysis indicator which generally generates

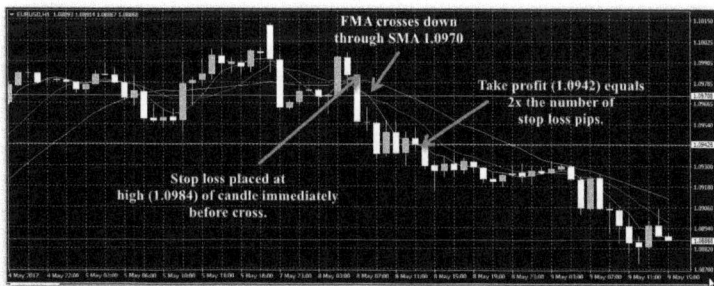

Figure 3.9 EUR/USD hourly chart

accurate buy-and-sell signals and normally has decent profit potential. However, I cannot overemphasize the importance of you creating a viable trading plan and above all not deviating from it.

Support and Resistance

Levels of support and resistance are one of the easiest concepts to understand in the context of both the forex markets and the stock markets. They define the points where the laws of supply and demand leads the price action as buyers and sellers come into the market. Support and resistance levels are areas where supply and demand is not in balance. When there are many buyers in the market, there is high demand for a currency pair which in turn creates a level of support in the market. Equally, when a high number of sellers enter the market, there is high supply which creates a level of resistance which prevents the price moving higher.

The level at which demand is strong enough to stop the price of a currency falling further is called the support level. The logic behind this is that as a price declines and the currency gets cheaper as there are less sellers and the price becomes more attractive to the buyers. Once enough buyers have entered the market, the price stops falling and bounces up generating a support level. When eventually the support level breaks, it very often becomes a new resistance level as investors use this level to place their stop losses. Figure 3.10 shows a support level on a NZD/USD daily chart.

Figure 3.10 NZD/USD daily chart

The support level on the NZD/USD chart is around the price of 0.6880. The price bounces off that level 15 times and breaches it for the first time in early May 2017. If you were trading this currency pair, you would be looking to buy at or near the significant areas of support to take advantage of the potential bounce off the support level.

Resistance is when a currency price meets a price barrier on its way up. It is at this level where more and more sellers enter the market and this stops the price from appreciating further. Very often it is also the level where buying interest fades as investors feel the currency is overpriced. At this level, the supply will become more than the demand and the price will bounce down off the newly created resistance level. Once the price breaks through this resistance level, it often then becomes a new support level. Once a breakthrough happens, the price very often surges onward as more and more investors enter the market to catch the action. Figure 3.11 shows resistance levels on a USD/CHF weekly chart.

As you can see there are two distinct areas of resistance on this chart. The first area is around the 0.9800 price level, which between February 2016 and September 2016 had the bulls trying to breach it but failing. Once breached, an upward trend saw the price hit a high in January 2017 before falling to the 0.9900 support level. It then attempted to breach the resistance at 1.0100. In fact, between January and April 2017 the price swung in a range between the 0.9900 support and the 1.0100 resistance level.

Horizontal lines and round numbers such as numbers with a trailing zero or with two trailing zeros are known as static support or resistance

Figure 3.11 USD/CHF weekly chart

Figure 3.12 USD/CAD weekly chart

levels. However, many traders use moving averages as dynamic support and resistance levels. Look at the USD/CAD weekly chart (Figure 3.12) where the 20-period SMA acts as a dynamic support and resistance level.

An arrow shows where a support area is located on the 20-period SMA, and another arrow shows a resistance area, and the white arrow another support area. I have also drawn a 50-period SMA, which sits below the 20-period SMA and which also shows a support and a resistance area indicated by arrows. To trade dynamic support and resistance levels, you should wait for the price to hit the level and then trade the bounce. You should buy on a support level price bounce and sell on a resistance level price bounce. In reality, do not expect prices to bounce upward the moment they hit a support level or drop down when they hit a resistance level, this rarely happens. The prices will break these lines as they "test" the levels and that "testing" is usually characterized by candlestick shadows.

If used, this can be a very successful strategy. Always keep in mind the phrase "the trend is your friend" and draw trend lines to help you analyze where the support and resistance levels probably lay.

Pivot Points

In the financial markets, the level at which the direction of the market changes is called the pivot point. This point is calculated using very simple mathematics utilizing the previous day's close, low, and high. The prices that are calculated form the resistance and support level pivotal points.

Table 3.2 Pivot point calculation on EUR/USD price chart

Category	Calculation	Price
Pivot	Previous day's close + low + high/3 =	1.1166
First resistance (R1)	2 × pivot point – low =	1.1223
First support (S1)	2 × pivot point – high =	1.1132
Second resistance (R2)	Pivot point + (high – low) =	1.1257
Second support (S2)	Pivot point – (high – low) =	1.1075
Third resistance (R3)	High + 2 × (pivot point – low)	1.1314
Third support (S3)	Low – 2 × (high – pivot point)	1.1041

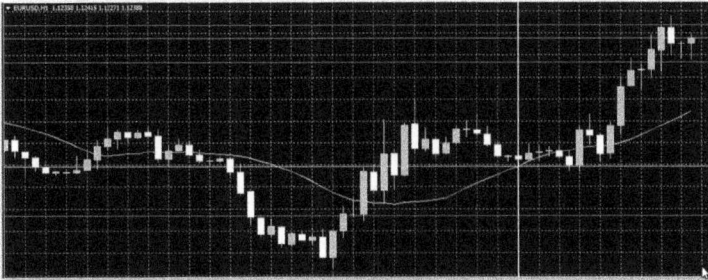

Figure 3.13 EUR/USD hourly pivot point chart

It is one of the simplest and most popular methods used by traders to forecast the market daily moves. The calculation has the specific function of showing where the market trends will be. Table 3.2 shows you how to calculate pivot points. We will assume a previous day's closing EUR/USD rate of 1.1188, a previous day's high of 1.1201, and a previous day's low of 1.1110.

I have drawn the pivot point and the resistance and support lines from Table 3.2 onto a EUR/USD daily chart and then changed the timeframe to hourly as shown in Figure 3.13. The most accurate time-frame for pivot point calculations is the daily high, low, and close, and once you have calculated these and drawn them onto the chart, you can then change the timeframe to hourly or even four hourly. The white horizontal line is the pivot and the vertical line of the same color indicates the beginning of the day that the pivot points have been calculated for. The darker horizontal lines above the pivot point indicate the resistance level prices with resistance (first) being the closest to the pivot point and the second resistance line at the top of the chart. The third resistance line is off the chart in this time frame. Similarly, the dark line below the pivot point indicates the support price levels with support (first) being the closest to the pivot point and support (third) being the furthest away.

As you can see from the chart, the pivot acts as a support area soon after the day's opening and it continued to act as a support level for several hours as the price action bounced off the support. The price then moved upward toward the first resistance line. The market was undecided hence the doji candle with a thin body, but then it moved up again before retracing from the second resistance line back toward the first resistance line, then bouncing off it twice. Note that the 20-period SMA also acts as a support and resistance level.

Traders trade pivot points in the same way they trade support and resistance levels. They look for the bounces off the levels. For example, looking again at the pivot point chart we see that the EUR/USD pair at the opening did not break below the pivot. So, you could have entered a buy trade with a stop loss at the price of the first support line. The price action then took the price up to the first resistance line, where, at that point you probably would have waited for the next candle to form to see if the price was going to retrace back toward the pivot or stall for a brief time. You would have seen the doji forming, indicating uncertainty and a market not sure where to go. However, the price moved up and broke through the first resistance line toward the second resistance line where it bounced off back to the first resistance line before bouncing between the first and second resistance lines for two or three candles. In fact, the price action continued to bounce between the two resistance levels for 10 hours before it breached the first resistance line and fell toward the pivot. In this scenario, you probably would have held your long position and only closed it once the breach of the first resistance line occurred.

In general, if at the beginning of the trading day the market is below the pivot point you should be looking for a sell and the price to break to the downside toward the first support level. If, on the other hand, the market is above the pivot point, you should expect to buy and a break toward the upside toward resistance level 1.

Fibonacci Retracements

A favorite trader's technical analysis tool is Fibonacci retracements or Fibonacci numbers. This tool is named after Leonardo Fibonacci who was a mathematician of Italian origin who created a series of numbers which traders use to help them to identify price support points and price resistance points for any time period the trader is interested in. Support points are the areas where prices have difficulty in breaking through when the market is falling and is in a bearish trend. Conversely, resistance points are areas where the price has difficulty in breaking through when the market is rising and there is a bullish trend.

The Fibonacci series of numbers begins with the numbers 0 and 1. The continuation of numbers in the series is calculated by the following number totaling the addition of the previous two numbers. The series is 0, 1, 1, 2, 3, 5, 8, 13, 21, 34, 55, 89, 144 till infinity. The relationship between this series of numbers is the number 1.618 or 16.18 percent. Therefore, if you take the number 34, for example, and multiply it by 16.18 percent you have the next number in the series which is 55. There is also a fixed relationship between the second number down from any number in the series. The relationship between those two numbers is 61.8 percent. So, for example, the second number down from 55 is 21, which is 61.8 percent of 55. The same fixed relationship is seen between the third number down from any other number in the series. For example, the number 13≈is 23.6 percent of 55. So, we have a series of relationships which looks like this: 23.6 percent, 38.2 percent, 50 percent, and 61.8 percent. These percentages represent the levels at which a currency price is most likely to retrace (reverse itself) before it continues its original trending bearish or bullish course. The 50 percent level is not really a Fibonacci number but traders use it because prices tend to reverse after retracing half the previous move.

All trading platforms have a tool that you can use to draw Fibonacci retracement levels. You can apply Fibonacci to your charts basically in a three-step process.

- You select a high and low point for a given up or downtrend
- Your charting software then calculates where a retracement of 23.6 percent, 38.2 percent, 50 percent, 61.8 percent, and 100 percent of that trend would occur, and
- It then draws in lines at those price levels.

I have drawn Fibonacci retracement levels on the EUR/USD 4-hour chart shown in Figure 3.14.

When drawing Fibonacci levels to identify the potential retracement levels for a downtrend, we use the previous uptrend by using its starting price and ending price level to draw the Fibonacci levels.

The Fibonacci levels are in effect support and resistance levels. As the chart shows, the EUR/USD price met resistance at the 100 percent level and moved upward until it stalled and met resistance at the 61.8 percent level. The price then moved up breaking through the 50.0 percent and 38.2 percent resistance levels before stalling and meeting resistance at the 23.6 percent level. The price then retraced back to the 50 percent support level where it reversed again and continued its upward movement until meeting resistance at the 0.00 percent level. The price then retraced back to the 23.6 percent support level where it tried to maintain upward momentum but bears pressure caused it to drop again to the 23.6 percent support level.

Now, if we wind forward a couple of days, we view the price action for days immediately following the EUR/USD chart shown in Figure 3.14. Now the EUR/USD chart (Figure 3.15) is showing that the price action moved up to the resistance level 0.00 percent before falling down to the 50.0 percent support level. It then retraced back to the 0.00 percent resistance before bouncing between the 23.6 percent and the 38.2 percent levels. It then broke through the 38.2 percent support level falling to the 61.8 percent support level then retracing back to and bouncing off the 38.2 percent resistance level.

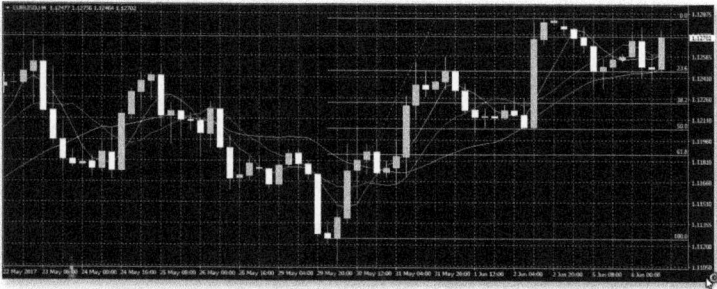

Figure 3.14 EUR/USD 4-hour chart

Figure 3.15 EUR/USD 4-hour chart

It is important to note that the Fibonacci lines represent levels and not exact points at which the price action rebounds, therefore the price action rarely rebounds exactly on the resistance or support lines, but just above or just below the lines. Also, lines can interchange between support and resistance levels. When the price action is moving upward, the lines are resistance levels and when the price moves downward, the lines become support levels. It is important that you draw the lines accurately so that you will be looking at the same support and resistance levels as other traders and therefore able to correctly trade the price retracements.

Let us see how we can identify trading opportunities using Fibonacci retracements. The USD/JPY daily chart in Figure 3.16 shows three possible trading opportunities.

The first opportunity is marked by arrow 1 which points to a bear candle in the area where the price retraced from the 38.2 percent line.

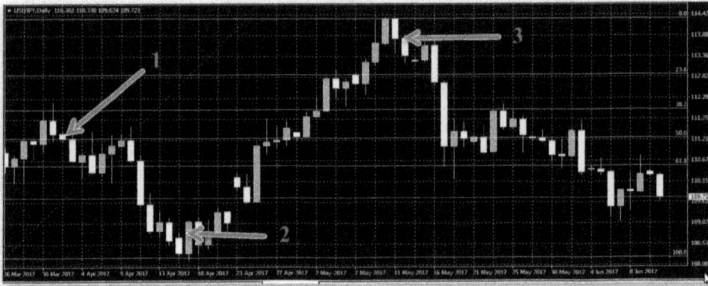

Figure 3.16 USD/JPY daily chart

Seeing that a bear candle was forming immediately after the initial re-tracement bear candle, you could execute a sell trade, setting a stop loss just above the 38.2 percent line at 112.10. The price then fell to 108.20 to the 100 percent line, a movement of 390 pips. As the price then bounced off this line, you would exit the sell trade and take the 390 pips profit from the trade.

An opportunity for a buy trade then presents itself as indicated by arrow 2. You would enter a buy trade and set your stop loss just below the 100 percent line at 108.00. The price moves up all the way to the 0.00 percent line before it starts to retrace again. You would close your buy trade with a profit of approximately 600 pips and then enter a sell trade halfway down the second bear candle as indicated by arrow 3. By the time the price had fallen to the last candle on the right-hand side of the chart, you would have made a profit of approximately 400 pips. You would stay with the trade until a likely retrace occurred, probably at the 100 percent line. However, whether you stay with the trade or not, up to that point you would have made over 1,000 pips profit on these three trades.

Using Fibonacci retracements as a guide for setting stop-loss prices will allow you to prevent major losses on your trades. As the price action moves up through each of the Fibonacci resistance levels, they then become support levels, and to lock in your profit, it is prudent for you to move your stop loss to just below the support level immediately below the current price. Conversely, if the price is falling through Fibonacci support levels, move your stop loss to just above the resistance level immediately above the current price.

The Fibonacci number sequences have been fascinating traders all over the world and although these numbers can be applied to many things, they have become very common as technical analysis tools with forex traders. Their popularity can be attributed to their uncanny accuracy in forecasting the movements in the forex market and so helping you to make more accurate decisions as to when to enter and exit the market. Using Fibonacci to trade the forex markets provides you with highly predictive tools which will enhance your market analysis skills, reduce your risk, as well as help you make larger profits.

Leading and Lagging Indicators

Before we talk about the most common and popular indicators, we should look at the difference between leading and lagging indicators and why indicators are so termed.

A leading indicator is strongest during periods of sideways or very small trending trading ranges, while the lagging indicators are regarded as more useful during trending periods but you need to make sure the indicator is heading in the same direction as the trend.

The leading indicators will create many buy-and-sell signals that make it better for choppy nontrending markets instead of trending markets where it is better to have less entry and exit points. Most of the leading indicators are oscillators, which are indicators that are plotted within a bounded range. An oscillator will swing between overbought and oversold conditions based on the preset levels of the specific oscillator.

A lagging indicator is an indicator that follows price movements and has less predictive qualities. Lagging indicators are more useful during distinct trending periods, however, during periods where there are no clear trends they are much less useful. This is the case because lagging indicators tend to focus more on the trend and produce fewer buy-and-sell signals. This allows you to capture more of the trend instead of perhaps being pushed out of your position because of the volatile nature of the leading indicators.

The two key ways that indicators are used to form buy-and-sell signals are through crossovers and divergence. Crossovers happen when the

Table 3.3 Leading and lagging indicators

Leading indicators	Lagging indicators
Relative strength indicator (RSI)	Moving averages
Stochastic oscillator	Bollinger bands
Commodity channel index	Moving average convergence divergence (MACD)
Williams percent range indicator	

indicator moves through an important level or a moving average of the indicator. It signals that the trend in the indicator is shifting and that this shift will lead to a change in the direction of the price of the currency pair or stock. The second way indicators are used is through divergence, which occurs when the direction of the price trend and the direction of the indicator trend are moving in the contradictory direction. This indicates that the direction of the price trend is probably weakening as the underlying momentum is changing.

Table 3.3 lists the most common leading and lagging indicators used by traders today, and all these indicators will be discussed in the following sections of this chapter.

Bollinger Bands

One of the simplest technical analysis tools to master is Bollinger Bands. This is an indicator used by many traders to improve their trading results in both the foreign exchange and stock markets. It was developed by John Bollinger and has become for many successful trader's their favorite technical analysis indicator. A Bollinger Band should not be used on its own to indicate buy or sell signals because that is not its function. It should be used in conjunction with other indicators in order to identify buy-and-sell signals. A Bollinger Band is made up of a middle band and two outer bands. The middle band is an SMA most commonly set at 20 periods and the outer bands are two standard deviations above and below the middle band. The look-back periods for the standard deviations also use an SMA which is the same number of periods as the middle band moving average. Figure 3.17 shows a GBP/USD hourly chart with a Bollinger Band indicator.

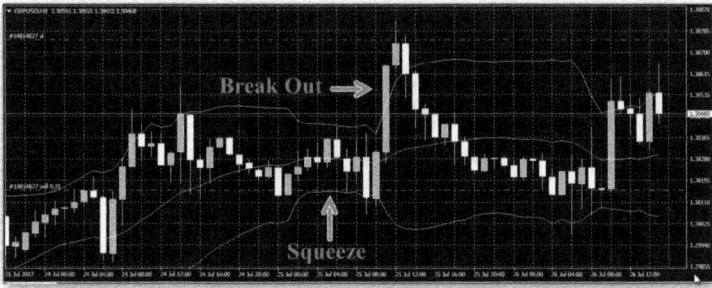

Figure 3.17 GBP/USD 1-hour chart Bollinger Band

The first thing you will notice is that the prices (candlesticks) move from one outer band to the opposite outer band or move from an outer band to the center band and then back out again. Also, the bands themselves can contract and squeeze the prices into a tight channel. I have indicated such a squeeze on the chart. The prices in a squeeze are ranging, indicating that there is little volatility in the market. However, as the prices break out (see my note on the chart) of their ranging period, the bands begin to widen indicating more and more volatility as the prices begin to climb or fall sharply.

When the price falls outside the bands, it is said to be "breaking the bands." As we have said, this occurs during times of extreme volatility and represents the strongest signal indicated by a Bollinger Band that a trend reversal is forthcoming. The way the Bollinger Band formula is constructed means that prices generally only break the bands about 5 percent of the time.

The situation whereby the prices break the buy (top) band is termed "overbought," and conversely it is called "oversold" when the prices break the sell (bottom) band. Both are recognized as market reversal signals (Figure 3.18).

In the previous example, you can see that the EUR/USD currency pair was trending upward until the point where three consecutive closes break the buy band barrier (circled) on the 26th July. This is a strong reversal signal that identifies a possible "sell" entry. The existence of price chart patterns such as double tops and double bottoms can also help you identify buy-and-sell opportunities. When a price reaches the

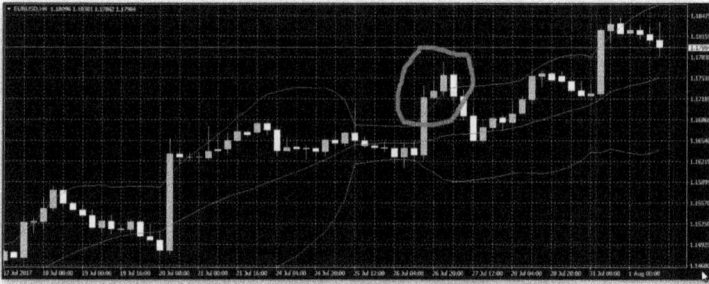

Figure 3.18 EUR/USD 4-hourly chart

Figure 3.19 EUR/GBP 1-hourly chart

maximum level that the market is willing to pay – the resistance level, the price frequently holds at that level, creating a second plateau more or less equal to the previous level. This is the second part of the double top and if the rally is to be extended, the second top will probably be slightly higher. If the subsequent top is lower, it is a signal that a price reversal is imminent as traders sell their positions or short the currency pair outright in anticipation of a drop in the exchange rate. A double bottom is basically the same as a double top but it is a signal that the support level for the price has been reached resulting in a price rise. Once the market is prepared to support the price from dropping further, more buyers enter the market in an attempt to buy into the currency pair at a low point just prior to an anticipated upswing. Figure 3.19 clearly shows an example of a double top and a double bottom.

The double top in the early evening of 31st July is circled in white and as you can see the price fell steadily through till 7 o'clock in the morning, where there was a false reversal before the price fell again and formed a double bottom (circled in white) at midday on 1st August. The price then reversed and rose steadily through 2nd August. If a trader like you decided to sell the EUR/GBP currency pair when the double top occurred, you would have made 25 to 30 pips on the trade assuming you bought back EUR/GBP at the double bottom. If you had also opened a EUR/GBP long position (buy) on the second candle of the double bottom, you would have made another 25 pips by the time the price had hit the top band.

There are several ways in which you can use Bollinger Bands. Whenever there is a bear or bull market, prices often retrace all the way back to the moving average. As a result, you can take advantage of this fact and enter the market when the price trend reverts to the general trend in the market.

Another way in which you can use a Bollinger Band is to take the appropriate position after the price has broken out of a narrow price channel. The Bollinger Band during a calm nonvolatile period would be quite narrow with the upper and lower bands close to the moving average. So once the price moves and the bands start to move away from the moving average, you can enter the market in the direction the price is heading and have a strong opportunity of a profitable trade (see Figure 3.20).

Third, when prices have reached either the upper limit of the Bollinger Band or the lower limit they will invariably retrace themselves back to the moving average line. Therefore, these movements offer you an opportunity to profit from the retracements.

Using a Bollinger Band as the sole technical analysis tool is not a recommended strategy. It is never wise to use one tool and there should

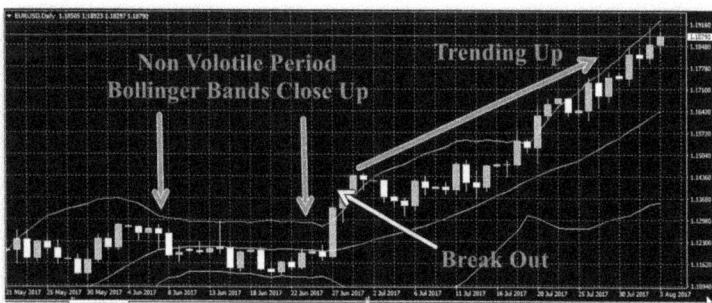

Figure 3.20 EUR/USD daily chart

always be another tool in your armory to confirm that a trading signal is more reliable. A tool which is a good fit with Bollinger Bands is the RSI. I will explain how it works and then show you how you can use it as a confirmation tool for not only Bollinger Bands but any other trend indicator.

Relative Strength Indicator

The relative strength index (RSI) is an analysis tool which is a momentum oscillator. The RSI is like the stochastic in that it identifies overbought and oversold conditions in the market. It was developed by J. Welles Wilder and it is a leading indicator that calculates the speed of change in price movements. The oscillator fluctuates between 100 and 0. Typically, market conditions are overbought when the oscillator's readings are above 70 and it indicates oversold market conditions when the readings are below 30.

On the chart (Figure 3.21), you will see the RSI indicator chart below the main candlestick chart area. Notice how the RSI line follows the same pattern as the price action. When the RSI line oscillates fairly equidistance between the 70 and the 30 lines, the price action is quiet and restricted to a narrow range around a support or resistance level. This you can see between March and August on the chart. Between April and June, the price was steadily coming down until in mid-June when the RSI line indicated the currency pairs were oversold when it dipped below 30. The price immediately began to rise, gaining momentum (steeper RSI line), until mid-November when the RSI line indicated an oversold condition

Figure 3.21 USD/JPY weekly chart

as it moved above 70. Upward momentum slowed and the price reversed its direction and started to come down. The RSI is confirming a bottom and then a top and in effect signaling a buy when it moves into oversold condition and a sell when it moves into an overbought condition. If you had bought 1 million dollars when the price was oversold, and sold when the price became overbought, you would have made over USD65,000 profit.

The RSI uses a 14-day period in its calculations. However, this can be changed according to your needs. If you prefer a more sensitive indicator, the 14 can be reduced, conversely for a less sensitive indicator you can increase the periods. A 10-period RSI is going to come to an overbought or oversold position a lot faster than a 20-period RSI. You can also change the readings so that an overbought condition is indicated above 80 rather than 70 or an oversold position is indicated below 20 rather than 30. Doing this would lessen the likelihood of trading too early on a false signal but it might also cause you to miss some profitable pips as the RSI would lag behind the market movement.

Now let us take our USD/JPY weekly chart again, add in a Bollinger Band and see how the RSI can be used as a confirming indicator.

As you can see, the RSI does indeed confirm the two trend reversals that take place between April 2016 and August 2017. The RSI is a good indicator for confirming entry or exit signals. As I have reiterated before, it is not an indicator that should be used alone but should be used together with a combination of at least one other indicator as I have shown in Figure 3.22.

Figure 3.22 USD/JPY weekly chart

Moving Average Convergence Divergence

The moving average convergence divergence (MACD) is a momentum indicator that is used to identify bullish or bearish trends. It displays the relationship between the moving averages of an assets price, whether it be stocks, currencies, or commodities.

In the left-hand top corner of the chart you can see three numbers. The number 12 represents the previous 12 bars of the faster moving average. The number 26 represents the previous 26 bars of the slower moving average. The number 9 represents the previous 9 bars of the difference between the two moving averages. This is plotted by vertical lines called a histogram as shown in Figure 3.

The MACD indicator charts momentum by measuring the increasing and decreasing space between two exponential moving averages (typically 12 days and 26 days). If the distance between the two moving averages is diverging, then momentum is increasing, whereas if the moving averages are converging, then momentum is decreasing. The distance between the two moving averages is graphed by what is called a MACD line, as seen in Figure 3.23. The changes in momentum are confirmed by a 9-day EMA added as a signal line (the dotted line in Figure 3.23). A buy signal is indicated when the MACD line crosses above the signal line. The sell signal is indicated when the MACD line crosses below the signal line.

On the chart in Figure 3.24, you can clearly see that between 9th June and 14th June there was convergence between the signal and MACD lines as the momentum of the downward price action slowed. Then a trend reversal took place and the signal line crossed above the MACD line indicating a potential buy signal on 14th June. Rising price momentum gathered pace and the signal and MACD lines diverged before converging once again as momentum slowed. On 14th July, the signal crossed below the MACD line indicating a sell signal. As the price action turned downward momentum

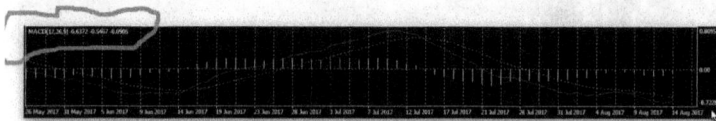

Figure 3.23 MACD indicator

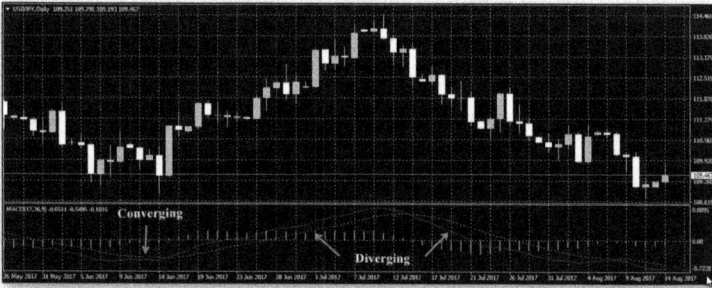

Figure 3.24 USD/JPY 1-day chart (MACD)

Figure 3.25 USD/JPY 1-day chart (three indicators)

gathered pace until around the 4th August the momentum slowed and the signal and MACD lines converged once again. It looked at the time that there might be a trend reversal coming up, however, that was not the case and the signal and MACD lines remained converged but did not cross.

As we have previously discussed, you should not use one indicator on its own but should use at least two others in conjunction with each other to confirm any buy-and-sell signals. So, in Figure 3.25 on the USD/JPY chart, we will use the RSI, which is considered a leading indicator, plus two EMAs, which are lagging indicators. The fast-moving average is set at 10 periods and the slow-moving average is set at 20 periods.

Now that we have three indicators on our chart (Figure 3.25), you should now be able to confirm if the MACD signals were false or not. The MACD buy signal occurred on the 15th June when the signal line crossed above the MACD line, however the two moving averages did not indicate a buy signal until the 19th June which was 4 days later. The RSI however, which is a leading indicator, signaled a buy on the 14th June, a day before the MACD did. The three indicators all gave a buy signal but on different days. So, if you had seen the RSI give a buy signal instead of trading on that signal, it would have been prudent to wait for a confirmation signal from the MACD or the moving averages. Both would have confirmed albeit on different days. It just depends on how risk averse your trading style is, whether you wait for all three indicators to confirm or you are quite happy to trade on the confirmation of a second indicator. Likewise, the sell signal on the MACD indicator on the 13th July was confirmed by the RSI on the 11th July and by the moving averages on the 20th July.

Commodity Channel Index

The commodity channel index (CCI) is a tool which was developed by Donald Lambert in 1980. It is used by traders to identify overbought or oversold conditions in the market or to give the trader a signal when a trend is losing strength. The CCI measures the difference between the average price change and the actual currency price change. A high reading indicates that prices are well above average which in turn indicates strength. On the other hand, a reading that is low shows that prices are below average and showing weakness. The CCI can be used in two ways. One way is as a co-incident indicator where strong moves above +100 is a sign of strong price action and a strong move below –100 is a sign of weak price action.

As a leading indicator, it reflects overbought and oversold positions which precede a reversion of the current price momentum. Most of the CCI movement takes places between the +100 and the –100 levels, and any movement that exceeds that range shows extreme weakness or strength. The best way of thinking about this is to think of the levels above +100 as bullish and the level below –100 as bearish. To avoid trading in market noise, it is advisable to trade when the move has passed through those levels.

Because the CCI does not have any limitations, identifying a true overbought or oversold position is at best subjective. Therefore, it is advisable to trade as the indicator approaches the +180 or the –180 levels. For lower timeframes, this level of movement is frequent but for higher timeframes, such as the daily chart shown in Figure 3.26, the frequency is low.

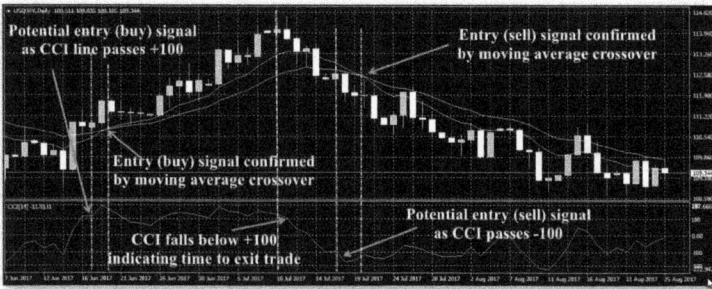

Figure 3.26 USD/JPN 1-day chart (CCI)

In the chart (Figure 3.26), I have indicated with a vertical white line and arrows where the CCI indicates possible entry or exit signals. The darker vertical lines and arrows indicate the confirmation of the signals by the moving averages crossovers.

On the 17th June, the CCI line passed through the +100 level moving toward the +180 region creating a potential buy signal. Two days later, the lagging moving average fast line crossed above the slow line (white) confirming a buy signal. The USD/JPY price trended up while the CCI line continued to stay close to the +180 zone. Finally, on the 10th July the CCI line began to drop below the +100 level indicating it was time to close out the long position as the USD/JPY was weakening. The pair continued to weaken and the CCI line dropped into the –100 area on the 16th July creating a potential sell signal. Three days later, the FMA line crossed under the slow-moving average line confirming the sell signal, and the USD/JPY continued to trend downward.

As we have seen from the chart, you should without fail confirm any potential trade signals with at least one more technical analysis tool. If you are using a leading indicator, confirm any potential trading signals with a lagging indicator to avoid trading into market noise.

Williams Percent Range Indicator

The Williams percent range indicator is another popular technical analysis tool with traders. It is a member of the oscillator family of technical analysis indicators. It was developed by Bill Williams and it has proven eerie in its ability to signal a reversal a couple of time periods ahead of the market. It is used by traders to define overbought and oversold conditions and market trend reversals. Its values move between zero and –100, and there are lines drawn at the –20 and the –80 values which act as warning signals of upcoming overbought or oversold positions. The values between –80 and –100 give very strong oversold condition and signal a buy. Conversely, the values between –20 and 0 give a very strong overbought condition and signal a strong sell. I also like to add another value to this indicator which is at the –50 level. When the indicator passes upward through the –50 line, I treat this as a buy signal if other indicators confirm a buy signal also. Conversely, when the indicator crosses downward through the –50 line, it is a strong sell signal which must be confirmed by at least one other indicator.

The chart in Figure 3.27 shows that on the 14th June, the Williams percent indicator signaled a potential reversal as the line moved into the oversold area. The line then moved up and passed through the –50 level on the 15th June signaling a strong buy. The buy was confirmed on the 19th June when the FMA crossed above the SMA. The Williams percent indicator stayed in the overbought area until the 11th July when it started to move out of the overbought level indicating a potential reversal. A strong sell signal was given on the 13th July as the indicator moved down through the –50 level. This signal was confirmed by the FMA crossing down through the SMA on the 19th July.

A few weeks later, on the 15th August there was an unconfirmed strong buy signal which proved to be a false trend reversing signal, instead it proved to be a short-term pull-back before the downward trend resumed.

Figure 3.27 USD/JPY 1-day chart

A profitable trading strategy which I use with the Williams percent range indicator is to always wait for a confirmation of the signals that the indicator gives out whether it is a buy or sell signal. However, I tend to look for a flattening of the moving average lines to indicate a potential exit point from the trade. Keeping to your trading strategy will ensure that you limit your losing trades and increase your profitable trades.

Stochastic Indicator

The stochastic oscillator is another forex chart technical tool that helps us determine where a trend might be ending. This particular momentum oscillator was created by George Lane in the late 1950s. A stochastic oscillator measures the momentum of price. If you imagine a ball going up in the air—before it can come down, it must slow down. Momentum therefore always changes direction before price.

While designed to follow the speed/momentum of price, it is also used to identify overbought and oversold conditions.

The two lines are similar to the MACD lines in the sense that one of the lines (blue) is faster than the other (red) line. As I have mentioned earlier, the stochastic oscillator tells us when the market is overbought or oversold and like all oscillators is scaled from 0 to 100. When the stochastic lines are above 80 (the silver dotted line in Figure 3.28), the market is overbought. When the stochastic lines are below 20 (silver dotted line), the market is oversold. As a rule of thumb, you buy when the market is oversold, and you sell when the market is overbought.

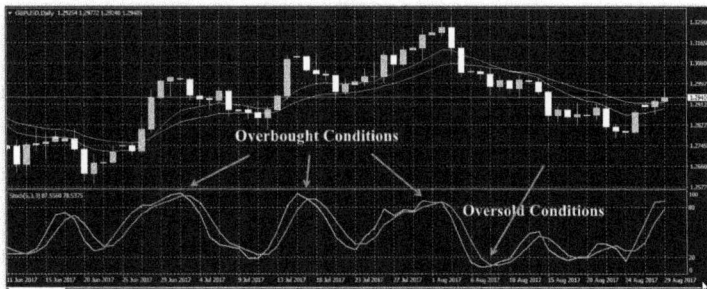

Figure 3.28 GBP/USD 1-day chart

Looking at the currency chart, you can see that the indicator has shown overbought conditions three times when both lines were above the 80 level. Each time the price action reversed and headed downward. The chart also shows one oversold condition where again the price reversed soon afterward. Interestingly, only one of the overbought conditions was confirmed by a moving average crossover and the single oversold condition was also confirmed by the moving averages – both much later than the price movement itself. So, using the moving averages as confirmation of a trade entry or exit would mean you missed out on a lot of profitable pips.

The stochastic oscillator also indicates buy-and-sell signals when the fast line crosses the slow line. Crossing up over the slow line is considered a buy signal and crossing down below the slow line is deemed a sell signal. In addition, the divergence of the two lines signals an increase in price momentum, whereas a convergence indicates price momentum weakening.

In Figure 3.29 we have used another leading indicator – the Williams percentage range – as a confirming tool to provide more precise trade entry and exit points. I have drawn a line to show the potential entry signal given by the stochastic oscillator, another line to show the confirming entry signal given by the Williams percentage range, and a white line to show the confirming entry signal given by the moving average. The white arrows indicate the buy signals and the dark arrows the sell signals.

Notice how the stochastic entry signals are given a few days earlier than the Williams percentage range which in turn gives entry signals a few days ahead of the moving average crossovers. This means that if you are very risk averse, you could wait for the moving average crossover, at

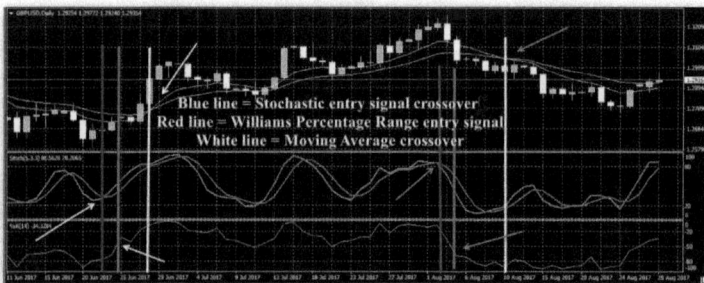

Figure 3.29 GBP/USD 1-day chart

which point you will have two confirmed entry signals. If you are less risk averse, you could trade on the entry signal confirmed by the Williams percentage range.

Traders use the stochastic indicator in different ways, but the main purpose of the indicator is to show us where the market conditions could be overbought or oversold. Over time, you will learn to use the stochastic oscillator to fit your own personal forex trading style.

Summary

In this chapter, we have looked at the most common and probably the most popular technical analysis tools that are available to you. All of them are available on the MetaTrader trading platform which is the platform you will most likely be using to trade on.

Price action in the markets can be very significant and have consistent movement either up or down, so it is very important that you recognize the trading opportunities that are presented. To successfully trade the opportunities that come along, you must have a rock-solid entry and exit strategy. To help make your strategies successful, you should develop a trading plan. This plan should include the following elements:

- The two or three technical analysis indicators you will use
- The conditions for a trade entry or exit
- Stop-loss and take-profit levels
- Maximum risk capital per trade (usually between 2 and 5 percent)

If you consistently keep to your trading plan, you should be able to make more successful trades than losing trades. Remember that no trader ever has a 100 percent success rate; however, if you are able to have more than 50 percent winning trades, it is a successful ratio.

CHAPTER 4

Fundamental Analysis

Your work as a trader will be done prior to the trade being executed. Traders spend huge amounts of their time in research and studying data they have produced from their technical analysis indicators or economic data that is coming over their news screens. Fundamental analysis is all about interpreting economic indicators, social factors, and government policies, and all three can have a significant influence on the price of a country's domestic currency.

The factors that a trader analyzes for fundamental analysis are interest rates, growth rates, inflation rates, and unemployment levels. These issues all impact on the supply and demand of a currency with interest rates and the overall strength of an economy (gross domestic product, GDP) being the two key factors influencing a currency. News stories can also affect the price of a currency which is why traders have news feeds from such agencies as Reuters, CNN, and Bloomberg, live on their screens. News events can have a dramatic short-term effect on a currency causing extreme volatility, particularly speeches by influential people such as governors of central banks, or economic ministers. This is why for a novice trader "trading the news" is not recommended because it could be such a disaster that the trader never recovers.

Economic Calendar

To help position themselves in the face of forthcoming news and economic events, traders keep an eye on the economic calendar which is published daily. Economic and political news can change the direction of a currency pair in seconds, and fundamentals that are true at an instance of time can be rendered absolutely meaningless by fresh fundamentals a few seconds later. The economic calendar enables traders to keep track of economic indicators and political events that impact currency movements.

The economic news for traders in the financial markets is programmed months in advance. Traders will know in advance when a meeting of the European Central Bank to discuss policy on interest levels will take place on a particular date in the future. This gives traders time to do some research and analysis and position themselves accordingly. All brokers publish a live economic calendar which updates almost immediately the economic data are released.

Take a look at the Economic Calendar for the September 1, 2017 (Figure 4.1).

As you can see, the calendar has seven columns.

Column 1—Time that the data are going to be released

Column 2—The currency affected by the news

Column 3—The event that will occur

Column 4—The volatility impact on the currency/market (the published economic calendar is shaded red for high volatility, orange for mild volatility and yellow for no volatility)

Column 5—The actual published data

Column 6—A consensus of the data

Column 7—Previously published numbers

GMT	Time left	Event	Vol.	Actual	Consensus	Previous
		FRIDAY, SEP 01				
08:00	✓	EUR Gross Domestic Product (QoQ) (Q2)		0.4%	0.4%	0.4%
08:00	✓	EUR Gross Domestic Product (YoY) (Q2)		1.5%	1.5%	1.5%
08:30	✓	GBP Markit Manufacturing PMI (Aug)		56.9	55.0	55.3
09:06	✓	EUR Gross Domestic Product n.s.a (YoY) (Q2)		0.8%		0.4%
12:30	✓	USD Labor Force Participation Rate (Aug)		62.9%		62.9%
12:30	✓	USD Unemployment Rate (Aug)		4.4%	4.3%	4.3%
12:30	✓	USD Average Hourly Earnings (MoM) (Aug)		0.1%	0.2%	0.3%
12:30	✓	USD Average Hourly Earnings (YoY) (Aug)		2.5%	2.6%	2.5%
12:30	✓	USD Average Weekly Hours (Aug)		34.4	34.5	34.5
12:30	✓	USD Nonfarm Payrolls (Aug)		156K	180K	189K
13:30		CAD Markit Manufacturing PMI (Aug)				55.5
13:45		USD Markit Manufacturing PMI (Aug)			52.5	52.5
14:00		USD Michigan Consumer Sentiment Index (Aug)			97.4	97.6
14:00		USD ISM Prices Paid (Aug)			62	62
14:00		USD ISM Manufacturing PMI (Aug)			56.5	56.3

https://www.fxstreet.com/economic-calendar

Figure 4.1 Economic calendar

On this calendar, there are several events that will have a big impact on the currency markets, all have been coded red. These are the U.S. unemployment figures, average hourly earnings, U.S. nonfarm payroll numbers, the ISM (Institute for Supply Management) prices paid, and the ISM manufacturing purchasing managers' index (PMI). The unemployment rate missed its target and was slightly higher than the forecast and last month's numbers. The average hourly earnings were down on both the forecast and last month's numbers. The nonfarm payrolls increased by 156,000, but this was a lot worse than the forecast and the previous month's number had been revised down also. These statistics all had a dramatic effect on the dollar, and as we can see from Figure 4.2 there were wild fluctuations in the markets in the span of half an hour.

The dollar initially lost 60 pips in a few minutes as the worse than forecast news was digested even though worse than expected. Then, as the overall trend for the United States was of a strengthening economy, the dollar recovered quite dramatically and gained 80 pips in a few short minutes. Imagine if you had bought dollars just before the figures were released and seeing the dollar weakening you closed out your losing position and traded again, this time selling dollars. You would then be staring at your screen in horror as the dollar dramatically strengthened and you had another losing trade on your hands. The lesson here is to never trade economic news either just before the news breaks or just after its broken. Always wait for the market to settle back down again.

Later in this chapter, there are explanations of the key economic data that cause short-term extreme volatility in the market. If you understand

Figure 4.2 EUR/USD 1-hour chart

what the data are and why it affect the markets, you should then be able to position yourself on the right side of the market once the immediate impact has settled down. Remember that short-term volatility does not mean a reversal in the trend.

Traders are constantly analyzing future economic events to try and understand before the announcement what the news might be. The consensus column on the economic calendar indicates the average estimate of all the analysis. Once this has been done, traders then place trades according to where they think the currencies will be when the announcement is released. By the time the announcement is made, traders have probably priced in the value of the currency pair. That is why when the released figure is the same as the consensus number, the market does not respond.

Trading the News

Economic news is one of the biggest drivers of short-term currency movements in the forex markets or in any other financial market for that matter. The currency markets respond very easily to economic news, especially the news coming out of the United States, as 80 percent of foreign exchange trading involves the dollar. But also, economic news coming from other major economies can dramatically affect their domestic currency.

Trading the news has become an accepted strategy in the forex markets in recent times. It is almost a regular occurrence to see currency pairs shift from 50 to 100 pips or more within a few seconds of a major economic news release. You are now probably thinking "that's got to be easy money," maybe it is or maybe it all depends on your preparation in anticipating the news release.

Trading on the release of economic news releases can be a major tool in your trading armory as long as you perform due diligence on the data and its potential impact on the markets. Economic news releases regularly stimulate strong short-term currency movements, which could offer big trading prospects for you, especially as the forex markets are open 24 hours a day over several time zones, so there are plenty of chances on nearly every trading day to grab a lot of pips driven by a news release.

Obviously, you can cherry-pick the currencies and news releases of the major economies which you want to concentrate on, however, because the dollar is the most traded currency, economic news coming out of the United States tends to bring about a marked reaction in the market.

Trading news is not as easy as it perhaps sounds. Both the consensus number and the revisions that come after publication are important. Also, some news is more significant than others; its importance depends on the economic size of the country where the data are being released and the significance of the news in relation to the other data being released on the same day.

The economic data that have a tendency to seriously affect price action in a currency are

- Interest rate decisions
- Retail sales
- Industrial production
- Inflation as indicated by consumer prices or producer prices
- Trade balance
- Unemployment
- GDP

In addition, surveys related to business, manufacturing, and consumer confidence are also significant. The comparative importance of the economic data may also change, as certain data may be more important this month than other data. Therefore, you should keep abreast of what is important to the market now.

As fundamental analysis, unlike technical analysis, is more of a long-term trading strategy, so when trading the news, your strategy should reflect that. Which is why I said earlier that you should not trade immediately prior or post a news release. Look at the long-term impact on the domestic currency of the economic data being published in the context of the significance of the news being better, worse, or what the market expects. This thought process will enable you to decide on the most profitable entry or exit strategy.

Initial Jobless Claims

The Initial Jobless Claims released weekly by the US Department of Labour is a measure of the number of people filing first-time claims for

| 12:30 ✓ | ▦ USD | Continuing Jobless Claims (Aug 18) | ▦ | 1.942M | 1.950M | 1.954M |
| 12:30 ✓ | ▦ USD | Initial Jobless Claims (Aug 25) | ▦ | 236K | 237K | 235K ⓘ |

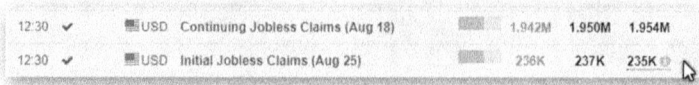

Figure 4.3 Initial jobless claims

state unemployment insurance. These statistics provide a measure of strength in the labor market. A larger than expected number indicates weakness in this market which influences the strength and direction of the U.S. economy. Largely speaking, a decreasing number should be taken as positive or bullish for the dollar, and conversely, higher claims indicate that the economy is weakening. The financial markets closely follow this number as it gives early warning on the direction of the economy (Figure 4.3).

When the unemployed in the United States have been out of work for more than 26 weeks, they move onto extended federal benefits and do not make weekly claims, so a reduction in claims might not accurately reflect the actual number of unemployed but show a better picture than exists in reality.

As jobless claims essentially ignore half of the unemployed, the financial markets look at two sets of data: the jobless claims and the extended claims. In reality, the extended claims are 1 week behind the jobless claims (continuing claims) so it is never 100 percent accurate, however it does give a more realistic picture.

Unemployment Rates

The unemployment rate released by the US Department of Labour is a percentage that is derived from dividing the number of unemployed workers by the total civilian labor force. It represents the percentage of people actively seeking employment and willing to work (Figure 4.4).

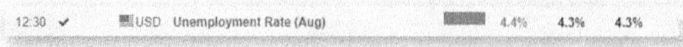

| 12:30 ✓ | ▦ USD | Unemployment Rate (Aug) | ▦ | 4.4% | 4.3% | 4.3% |

Figure 4.4 Unemployment rate

In general, a higher rate is seen as a weakening/recessionary economy, while on the contrary, a growing economy sees its unemployment rate decreasing. Therefore, a decrease of the figure is seen as bullish for the USD, while an increase is seen as negative (or bearish), although by itself the number cannot determinate the markets move, as it depends on the headline numbers of the nonfarm payroll.

Nonfarm Payroll

The nonfarm payrolls released by the US Department of Labour shows the number of new jobs created during the previous month, in all non-agricultural business. The monthly changes in payrolls can be extremely volatile, due to its close relationship with economic policy decisions made by the Central Bank.

The number is also subject to strong revisions (a circle indicates a revised number) in future months which also tends to trigger volatility in the forex market. Generally speaking, a high reading is seen as positive (or bullish) for the USD, while a low reading is seen as negative (or bearish), although previous month's revisions and the unemployment rate are as relevant as the headline figure, and therefore market's reaction depends on how the market assesses them all.

Consumer Price Index

The Consumer Price Index (CPI) Ex-Food and Energy is released by the US Department of Labour Statistics and is a measure of price movements through the comparison between the retail prices of a representative shopping basket of goods and services. Volatile products such as food and energy are excluded in order to capture a more accurate and smoother calculation. Generally speaking, a high reading is seen as positive (or bullish) for the USD, while a low reading is seen as negative (or Bearish) (see Figures 4.5 and 4.6).

https://www.fxstreet.com/economic-calendar

Figure 4.5 Nonfarm payroll

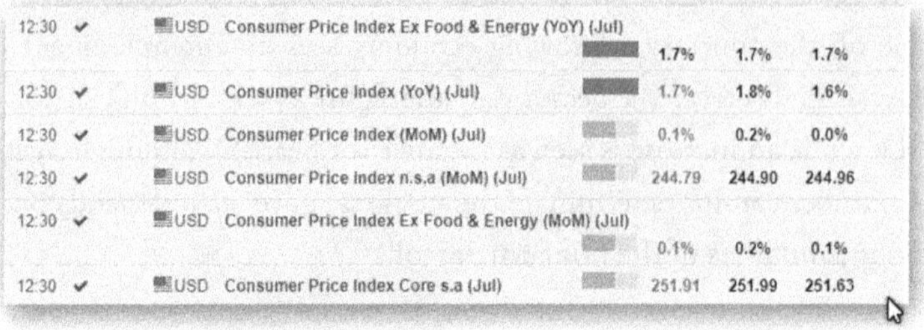

12:30	✔	USD Consumer Price Index Ex Food & Energy (YoY) (Jul)				
				1.7%	1.7%	1.7%
12:30	✔	USD Consumer Price Index (YoY) (Jul)		1.7%	1.8%	1.6%
12:30	✔	USD Consumer Price Index (MoM) (Jul)		0.1%	0.2%	0.0%
12:30	✔	USD Consumer Price Index n.s.a (MoM) (Jul)		244.79	244.90	244.96
12:30	✔	USD Consumer Price Index Ex Food & Energy (MoM) (Jul)				
				0.1%	0.2%	0.1%
12:30	✔	USD Consumer Price Index Core s.a (Jul)		251.91	251.99	251.63

https://www.fxstreet.com/economic-calendar

Figure 4.6 Consumer price index

The CPI is an important economic indicator (reported monthly 2 weeks after the reporting month), because it measures adjustments up or down in the selling prices consumers pay for goods and services. As such, it is a valuable early indicator of inflation. Inflation is a sign that the purchasing power of a country's currency is in decline and each unit of local currency buys fewer goods and services. A rise in inflation has a very negative effect on a currency. The producer price index (PPI) which feeds into the CPI controls inflationary trends and prevents the local currency from depreciating too much. If a local currency becomes less valued because of inflationary pressure, the demand for that currency decreases. This is especially evident if the country in question imports a high amount of goods and commodities that are considered valuable and needful from a country that has low production costs. These goods become more expensive as the local currency declines against the exporter's currency and the inflation rate rises in tandem as prices increase.

Markit Manufacturing PMI

The Manufacturing PMI released by Markit Economics captures business conditions in the manufacturing sector. As the manufacturing sector dominates a large part of total GDP, the manufacturing PMI is an important indicator of business conditions and the overall economic condition in the United States.

Points above 50 imply the economy is expanding and investors see this as bullish for the USD, whereas a result below 50 points indicates an economic contraction, and weighs negatively on the currency and is seen as bearish for the USD (Figure 4.7).

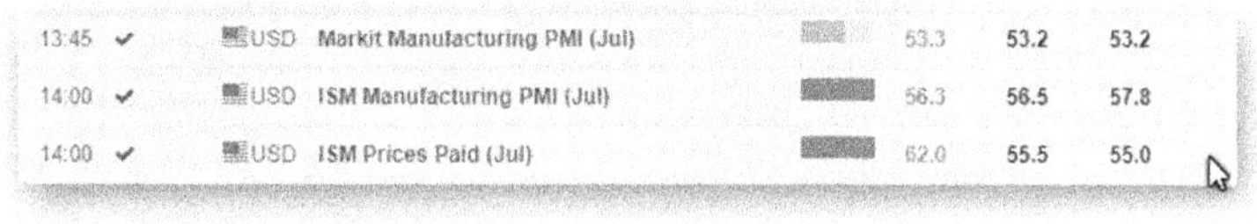

13:45 ✓	USD Markit Manufacturing PMI (Jul)	53.3	53.2	53.2
14:00 ✓	USD ISM Manufacturing PMI (Jul)	56.3	56.5	57.8
14:00 ✓	USD ISM Prices Paid (Jul)	62.0	55.5	55.0

Figure 4.7 Markit manufacturing PMI

ISM Manufacturing PMI

The Institute for Supply Management (ISM) Manufacturing Index shows business conditions in the U.S. manufacturing sector. It is a significant indicator of the overall economic condition in the United States. A result above 50 is seen as positive (or bullish) for the USD, whereas a result below 50 is seen as negative (or bearish).

Retail Sales Ex Autos

The Retail Sales ex Autos released by the US Census Bureau is data published monthly that show all goods sold by retailers based on a sampling of retail stores of different types and sizes except for the automobile sector. The retail sales index is often taken as an indicator of consumer confidence. This report is the "advance" report, which can be revised fairly significantly after the final numbers are calculated. Positive economic growth anticipates bullish movements for the USD, whereas negative economic growth is inclined toward a bearish reaction for the USD.

Retail Sales

The Retail Sales released by the US Census Bureau measures the total receipts of retail stores. Monthly percent changes reflect the rate of changes of such sales. Changes in Retail Sales are widely followed as an indicator of consumer spending. Generally speaking, a high reading is seen as positive (or bullish) for the USD, while a low reading is seen as negative (or bearish).

It is revised quite considerably after the final figures are calculated. Traders and analysts prefer to look at the retail sales figure "ex auto" which

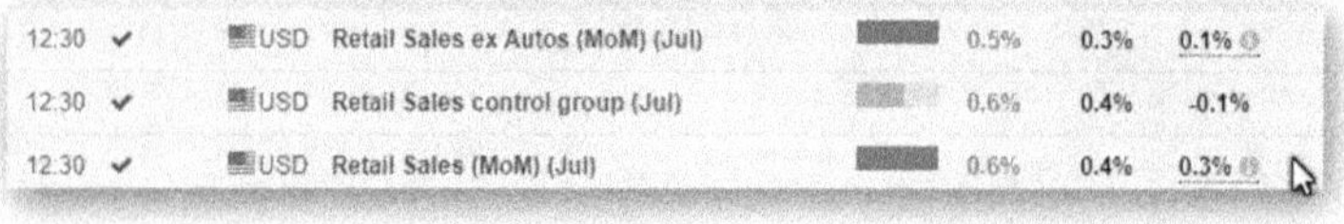

12:30 ✔	🔳USD	Retail Sales ex Autos (MoM) (Jul)	▬▬	0.5%	0.3%	0.1% ⊘
12:30 ✔	🔳USD	Retail Sales control group (Jul)	▬	0.6%	0.4%	-0.1%
12:30 ✔	🔳USD	Retail Sales (MoM) (Jul)	▬▬	0.6%	0.4%	0.3% ⊘

Figure 4.8 Retail sales

means that the numbers exclude car sales because they are expensive items and distort the final figure. The number without the car sales is considered a better measure of retail sales trends (Figure 4.8).

The report manages to capture the retail sales on a broad front and includes in-store sales as well as mail order sales and other out-of-store sales such as the Internet. It is broken down into several categories such as food, beverages, and clothing.

In addition, the retail sales are also a large constituent of total GDP and any long-term reduction in retail sales could signal a pending recession with a reduction in VAT receipts and company head counts. The retail sales figure is also fairly current as they can be collected quickly and provide data that are only a couple of weeks old.

The forex market finds the retail sales figure a difficult animal to analyze. Europeans and Asians like to see Americans in a buying mood because that can strengthen interest rates which are good for the dollar (bullish). However, too strong retail sales could be detrimental to the dollar because many goods are imported and that means there is demand for nondollar currencies to pay for the foreign goods. Weak retail sales could spell a recession and that too is not good for the dollar.

FOMC Minutes

FOMC stands for the Federal Open Market Committee that organizes eight meetings in a year which review economic and financial conditions in the United States. It also determines the appropriate stance of monetary policy and assesses the risks to its long-run goals of price stability and sustainable economic growth. FOMC Minutes are released by the Board of Governors of the Federal Reserve and are a clear guide to the future U.S. interest rate policy (Figure 4.9).

Figure 4.9 FOMC minutes

When it comes to the markets, the impact of interest rates and the effects are far broader than just the level of a mortgage rate. The interest rates that investors are particularly interested in are the interest rates which are set by the central banks of countries, particularly the interest rate set in the United States by the Federal Reserve. Central banks tend to use interest rates to stop an economic scenario where there is too much money chasing after too little produce and this leads to inflation in prices. By reducing or increasing the amount of money available for purchasing produce/goods a central bank can control inflation.

By increasing the interest rates, a central bank attempts to reduce the supply of money by making it more expensive to obtain. An interest rate increase does not have an immediate effect on the markets. What happens immediately however is that it suddenly becomes more expensive for banks to borrow money from the central banks. Banks in their turn increase the interest rates that they charge for lending money to their customers. Credit card and mortgage interest is increased particularly if they are not a fixed rate but have a variable rate. As people start to feel the effect of less money being around, they have less disposable income and are only able to spend money on bills which themselves have become more expensive. This in turn affects businesses ability to earn revenues and increased profits.

Gross Domestic Product

The GDP Annualized released by the US Bureau of Economic Analysis displays the monetary value of all the goods, services, and structures produced within a country in a given period of time. GDP Annualized is a gross measure of market activity because it indicates the pace at which a country's economy is growing or decreasing (Figure 4.10).

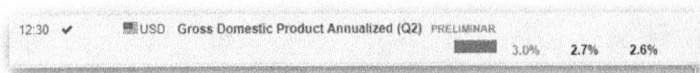

https://www.fxstreet.com/economic-calendar

Figure 4.10 GDP

Generally speaking, a high reading or a better than expected number is seen as positive (bullish) for the USD, while a low reading is negative (bearish).

Consumer Sentiment Reports

The Index of Consumer Sentiment (ICS) is an economic survey which is published monthly by the University of Michigan. It is designed to measure the consumer's confidence in the U.S. economy.

Two-thirds of expenditures and production in the economy of the United States is dedicated to private consumption and consumer spending. This includes such things as retail sales, utilities, medical health care, and rent. This is a very big sector of the economy and the accuracy of the numbers have an effect on some other key numbers which economists focus on, such as interest rates, employment, and inflation. The ability of a consumer to spend is indicated through the income, interest rates, and wealth, therefore comparing all these variables with the ICS can indicate what level of expenditure the consumer is likely to spend in the future. Any dramatic swing of confidence could cause a short-term spike in the markets.

Crude Oil Prices

Countries such as the United States, the Euro-zone countries, Japan, and India are extremely dependent on the crude oil price. If crude oil prices increase, these countries will see an increase in their imports, which in turn, as oil is priced in dollars, leads to an increase in the sales of their respective currencies, and a decrease in its value.

A Country's Political Condition

A country that has a stable government indicates to investors that the policies both economic and social are consistent and directed toward a growing GDP. This type of environment also leads to a stable currency. However, if a country has an unstable government and a series of general elections, this indicates uncertainty for the government's economic policies and often has a negative impact on the value of the country's domestic currency.

Price of Gold

The fluctuations in the price of gold can have a sudden impact on the domestic currencies of the countries which are the main producers as well as exporters of gold. The two major exporters of gold in the world are Canada and Australia, so if the price of gold rises, their currencies will tend to appreciate as gold buyers purchase their currencies to pay for the gold. In contrast, the countries who are net importers of gold will find their domestic currencies declining in value as the price of gold goes up.

Quantitative Easing

You only have to open a financial newspaper today to see the words "quantitative easing" and turn on a financial news channel to hear someone welcoming it or saying that it would not work. What is quantitative easing and why is it so dramatic? Actually, it is dramatic because in a nutshell it means creating gigantic amounts of money from nothing in the hope that the economy gets back on track. Many economists think that when you want to pick up the economy you must get more money into circulation. Unfortunately, there are very few ways in which this can be done.

One way is for the government to spend money by recompensing people to build things such as roads or factories or stadiums. That would certainly get more money into people's pockets. However, this is not a politically popular idea. It can be done once but not repeated.

Another way is for the Federal Reserve to reduce interest rates, which then makes it cheaper to borrow money. The theory being that people borrow more, and therefore purchase more, and build more original things. That has already happened when the Federal Reserve pulled interest rates all the way down to zero. You cannot go any lower than that.

These two tools have been used throughout economic history as we know it, either government spending or cutting interest rates. However, if these methods do not work, then the last resort is quantitative easing.

So how does quantitative easing work? Essentially, the Federal Reserve says that it is willing to buy up government securities held by banks for a little more than anyone else is willing to pay. The banks obviously like that and sell the bonds they are holding to the Federal Reserve. Now the banks have a cash pile of billions of dollars. But where did that money come from? That is the magic that the Federal Reserve or any other central bank can do. The money comes out of a hat. In other words, they invent it electronically.

So now the banks have billions of dollars. The Federal Reserve is hoping that the banks will decide to lend the money to companies and people to invest or buy things. This in turn stimulates the economy. This sounds like a win situation for everyone, however there are many economists who believe that quantitative easing does not work and it is too early to say if it is working this time. In the meantime, the United Kingdom and Europe are following the same strategy to stimulate their economies. At this point in time it seems to be working and the American economy is showing strong growth. Despite some economists having reservations, many other economists say that it is better than doing nothing and far better than austerity.

All the data and statistics that I have mentioned so far in this chapter can have a significant effect on the price action of the U.S. dollar. However, these same statistics and data also have a similar effect their particular countries domestic currency volatility. Take a look at an extract of the economic calendar for the September 8, 2017 (Figure 4.11).

At 8:30 a.m. the Consumers Inflation Expectations report was released in the United Kingdom. This is a report issued by the Bank of England which shows the percentage that consumers expect the cost of goods and services to change over the next 12 months. It can cause quite volatile price action for the GBP as the dark bar indicates (Figure 4.12).

FRIDAY, SEP 08						
08:30 ✓	🇬🇧 GBP	Consumer Inflation Expectations		2.8%		2.8%
09:00 ✓	🇪🇺 EUR	Consumer Price Index (YoY) (Aug)		0.9%	1.1%	1.0%
09:00 ✓	🇪🇺 EUR	Consumer Price Index - Harmonized (YoY) (Aug)		0.6%	0.9%	0.9%
09:00 ✓	🇪🇺 EUR	Industrial Production (YoY) (Jul)		1.7%		1.8% ⓘ
10:00 ✓	🇪🇺 EUR	Global Trade Balance (Jul)		€-3.461B		€-3.670B
12:00 ✓	🇬🇧 GBP	NIESR GDP Estimate (3M) (Aug)		0.4%		0.2%
12:30 ✓	🇨🇦 CAD	Net Change in Employment (Aug)		22.2K	19.0K	10.9K
12:30 ✓	🇨🇦 CAD	Participation rate (Aug)		65.7%		65.7%
12:30 ✓	🇨🇦 CAD	Unemployment Rate (Aug)		6.2%	6.3%	6.3%
12:30 ✓	🇨🇦 CAD	Capacity Utilization (Q2)		85.0%	84.9%	83.3%
12:45 ⟳	🇺🇸 USD	FOMC Member Harker Speech SPEECH				
14:00 1h 12m	🇺🇸 USD	Wholesale Inventories (Jul)			0.4%	0.4%

https://www.fxstreet.com/economic-calendar

Figure 4.11 Economic calendar

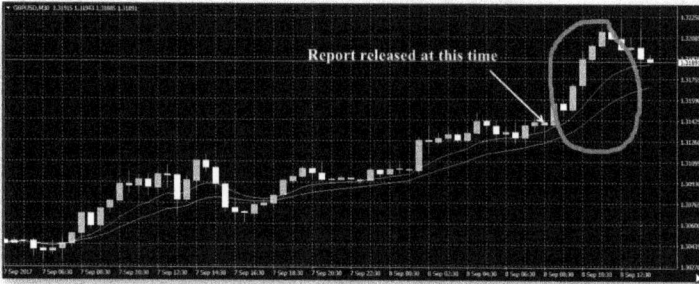

Figure 4.12 GBP/USD 30M chart

However, the actual number as compared with last month's figure was the same, and the market's reaction was very subdued for half an hour although later in the morning the GBP did strengthen by 80 or so pips.

Also on the same day at 12:30 p.m., the Net Change in Employment and the Unemployment Rate were released in Canada. Both numbers could have a major impact on price action and the bars are coded dark accordingly. The Net Change in Employment actually was a little better than expected and the Unemployment Rate was slightly down on the

Figure 4.13 USD/CAD 5M chart

forecast. Both results were considered positive for the Canadian dollar, and you might have expected the Canadian dollar to appreciate. If you had traded supporting your sentiment, you would have made a bad trade because as you can see from Figure 4.13, the Canadian dollar spiked in favor of the U.S. dollar on the release of the figures. It then came back to the price it was at immediately before the news was released.

In fact, the Canadian dollar had been doing well in long term since the interest rate hike in June, up to the release of the statistics, which indicates that the news was already priced into the rate. The dollar bulls took control after that and the Canadian dollar started a weak trend as rumors that the Bank of Canada does not foresee another rate hike anytime soon.

Notice that there were other economic data affecting the EUR and GBP that day, which did not have any significant effect on those currencies and were not expected to, as the volatility bars were shaded much lighter (no volatility) than dark and lighter than dark (mild volatility).

The Canadian dollar spike on the release of the employment numbers is a good example of the dangers of trading the news just before or just after the release of data. You cannot preempt the market unless you are very lucky, so do not take the risk. Position yourself prior to the news event making sure you have the appropriate stop losses in place in case of a spike against you. Or, wait until the market has settled back down before you trade. Fundamental analysis is important to understand in conjunction with technical analysis, however fundamental analysis sometimes has dramatic short-term effects on price action which can wipe out all your hard-earned profits.

CHAPTER 5

Trading Other Asset Classes

This chapter describes the asset classes (stocks, indices, contract for differences (CFDs), options, commodities) which can be traded online through a broker's trading platform as well as futures which can only be traded on an exchange through a broker. We will look at the key characteristics of each asset class as well as their usage to hedge open positions. It also describes the fundamental risks associated with the assets and instruments and how these risks can be mitigated. Trading tips designed to improve your ability to consistently make money are explained and analyzed. The instruments described in this chapter offer an alternative trading practice to that of the foreign exchange markets, however the technical analysis and fundamental analysis techniques described in earlier chapters in this book very much apply to trading these other asset classes.

Stocks/Equities

The stock market, unlike the forex market, is based on businesses and products that are established in individual countries. Also unlike the forex markets, the stock markets have set business hours. These hours are from 8 a.m. to 5 p.m., Monday to Friday, and they are normally closed on the banking holidays and weekends of the country they are situated in. The stock market is a market that is local to a country and its trading instruments are related to companies that are registered inside that country, although companies can be registered on more than one stock market.

A stock market is a place where organizations and individuals can trade stocks. It is a meeting place for buyers and sellers, and to acquire a stock, money must change hands from the buyer to the seller. To trade on a stock market, you must be registered with the stock exchange, which is why individuals and organizations trade through a stock broker who is listed on the exchange. When you buy shares in a company you also own a piece of the company in proportion to the number of shares you bought as well as gaining voting rights. You may also be entitled to share in a proportion of the company's profits through the issuance of dividends.

Stock trading can be conducted either online on a broker's trading platform or face to face with a broker. Like forex traders, stock traders use fundamental and technical analysis to decide on when to buy or sell their stocks. However, both fundamental and technical analysis of a stock involves very detailed analysis of the company that issues the stock and the industry or economic segment that the company does business in. Whereas forex traders tend to do all the analysis leg work themselves, stock traders tend to rely on third-party stock analysts' reports as part of their analytical process.

A stock price is quoted as a two-way price—bid and offer—as with forex prices, you buy the offer price and sell the bid price. Table 5.1 displays the prices of some popular stocks as of September 11, 2017.

There are two types of stock investors: the long-term investor and the short-term investor. In the main, the long-term investor invests in stocks and takes delivery of a stock certificate, pays commission fees, and stamp duty. The short-term investor is likely to be like you, a retail stock investor

Table 5.1 Popular stocks

Stock	Bid	Offer
Facebook	172.90	173.24
Tesla	357.54	357.81
Apple	161.09	161.43
Goldman Sachs	221.03	221.51
VeriFone	20.52	20.60

who buys stocks online through one of the many regulated online brokers using a leveraged product called a CFD. This instrument enables you to invest in a selection of major stocks with a reasonable leverage, which is the amount of margin you will pay to purchase your shares. Later in this chapter, we will discuss CFDs in detail.

Everywhere you look on the Internet or in the financial periodicals, you will find so-called gurus writing thousands of words on unfailing ways to pick stocks. Most articles are not well-written and even more disturbing, not well-researched. Unfortunately, the majority of articles could lead you down a dangerous road where you are likely to lose everything. The way to pick stocks is to use the tried and trusted methods that have been used successfully through bull and bear markets for years. Here are a couple of pointers.

One of the key things for a successful trade is to pick the right company as well as the right stock. Over time a stock's ratings will change, so it is imperative that you check its rating now and again. Invest in stocks that have recently been upgraded and try to avoid stocks that have been freshly downgraded. Recently, upgraded stocks have on average been giving a return of 10 percent plus annually, which is over 3 percent better than the overall average. Those stocks, which have been recently downgraded, have an average annual return of less than 1 percent, which is over 6 percent worse than average. A rating of one or less is considered a good buy. You can see the ratings of stocks from any number of Internet stock watch sites.

Another important number to look at is the price earnings ratio (PE ratio). This ratio is computed by dividing the annual earnings by the number of outstanding shares in the market. The average PE ratios of companies on the stock exchanges is 24 to 25 and anything higher than that would be considered a growth stock and a strong buy.

However, apart from using stock rating sites on the Internet similar to Figure 5.1 as guidelines to choosing a stock to buy, you must also do the due diligence necessary on the fundamental analysis of the companies whose stocks you are buying, to ensure that your trades give you decent profits.

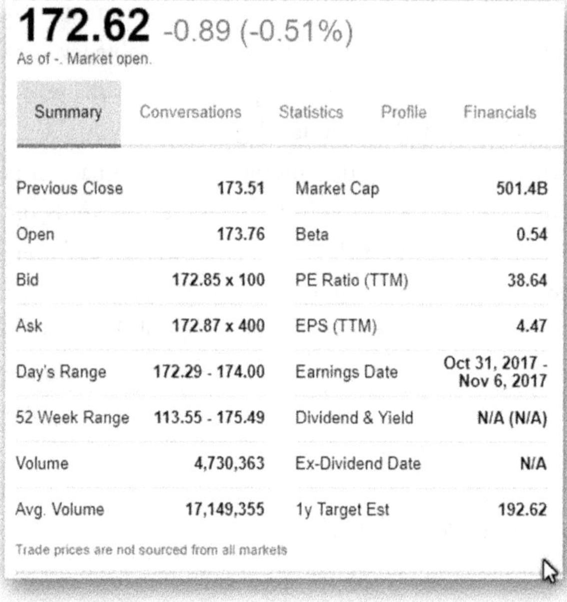

172.62 -0.89 (-0.51%)
As of -. Market open.

Summary	Conversations	Statistics	Profile	Financials

Previous Close	173.51	Market Cap	501.4B
Open	173.76	Beta	0.54
Bid	172.85 x 100	PE Ratio (TTM)	38.64
Ask	172.87 x 400	EPS (TTM)	4.47
Day's Range	172.29 - 174.00	Earnings Date	Oct 31, 2017 - Nov 6, 2017
52 Week Range	113.55 - 175.49	Dividend & Yield	N/A (N/A)
Volume	4,730,363	Ex-Dividend Date	N/A
Avg. Volume	17,149,355	1y Target Est	192.62

Trade prices are not sourced from all markets

Figure 5.1 Stock rating

Stock Markets/Indices

Wherever you turn nowadays, the mass media is sure to be commenting on the stock markets. Such phrases as "the market is up today by one percentage," or "the market fell on the news of weak economic growth in the United States." What is this market that the mass media are talking about? Well, what they are really talking about are indices.

Around the world, there are several important indices (Table 5.2):

What exactly is an index? It is a measurement of the changes in a pool of stocks which represent a segment of the market. As it is much too

Table 5.2 World indices

USA stock exchanges	Europe's stock exchanges	Far East's stock exchanges
Dow Jones Industrial Average	FTSE 100	Hang Seng (Hong Kong)
Standard & Poor's 500	DAX (Germany)	Nikkei (Tokyo)
NASDAQ	CAC (France)	China A50

difficult to follow every single stock traded in a market, a small segment of the market is taken that is as much as possible representative of the total market. In an ideal world any change in the price of an index mirrors an exact comparative change to the stocks which are in the index.

The first ever index was devised by Charles Dow back in 1896. The index then only had 12 stocks in it, but they were 12 of the largest companies in the United States. Before computers, indices were calculated by summing the stock prices of the companies in the index and then dividing by the number of companies in the index. This was of course no more than a simple average; however, it served its purpose quite well. Nowadays, indices use a one of two types of methodologies. The least popular is the index based on price-based weighting. In this methodology, the weight of each stock is the stock's price relative to the total of all the security prices. This system works well until a company does a stock split and although nothing changes fundamentally in the company, the weight is changed.

The most popular methodology is based on the company's market capitalization. A company's market capitalization is taken as a percentage of the total value of the stocks in the index. Therefore, if a company has a market capitalization of 10 million dollars and the value of all the stocks in an index is 500 million, the company is worth 2 percent of the index. With the calculations being done by computers, the calculations are very accurate and almost instantaneous, so they very accurately reflect the market.

Indexes tell us where the market is going and what the likely trend is. Investing in an index is of course much easier and cheaper than investing in every stock in the index itself. Although investing in an index does not guarantee that you will make money, historically returns on indices have been in the region of 10 percent. It just takes a little patience over the long term to see a return on your capital.

As we have mentioned, to trade efficiently it is important to have a liquid market, a complete understanding of the market, as well as knowledge of the economic indicators. A stock market investor in addition to performing due diligence on the stocks of interest, can also use the indicators to gauge the prevailing economic condition, thus enabling them to trade profitably and avoid potential losses.

As we have learnt there are numerous economic indicators, however there are essentially only four basic indicators that investors keep an eye on and pay a lot of attention to.

First, inflation is a vital economic indicator and very important to all investors. It determines the rate of returns that an investor obtains from a particular investment. Inflation's effect on the stock market is particularly complicated. This is because a company's or an investor's return is largely affected by high inflation. When input costs increase, the impact on the stock markets also increases gradually, depending on the incremental costs that a company passes onto its clients.

If inflation is accompanied by an increase in interest rates, the stock market is bound to suffer negatively. This is attributed to the fact that the bond markets are often viewed as a cheaper investment vehicle than stocks. In this case, investors will most likely sell their stocks and invest in bonds.

Second, the CPI is usually used as the indicator of inflation. Baskets of products such as food, housing, cars, clothes, and transport are the components of the price index. The total price of these goods is compared with the total price of what consumers consumed in the previous year. Any percentage increase could mean that inflation is picking up and the stock market will be negatively affected. However, a decrease in prices affects the stock markets positively.

Third, the GDP data are also key economic indicator. It refer to the total amount of goods and services that is being produced in a country during the specific period that is being measured. GDP is published quarterly and it reveals whether a country's economy is growing or not. It is a crucial indicator and if the GDP is positive, stock markets will also be positive. They will react positively therefore boosting investor's confidence. It also means that companies enjoy improved economic performances. On the other hand, if GDP contracts, consumers are forced to reduce spending, hence affecting the performance of companies negatively and consequently putting more pressure on stock markets.

Fourth, the labor market is similarly a key economic indicator which affects the stock markets. This essentially refers to the unemployment rate. The percentage of unemployment rate in a country reflects a country's economic state. In essence, when a country experiences an economic

Table 5.3 Investor reaction to indicator's movements

Economic indicator	Indicator	Stock investors	Bond investors	Dollar investors
GDP	Up	Buy	Sell	Buy
	Down	Sell	Buy	Sell
Unemployment	Up	Sell	Buy	Sell
	Down	Buy	Sell	Buy
Consumer Price Index	Up	Buy	Sell	Buy
	Down	Sell	Buy	Sell
Inflation	Up	Sell	Buy	Buy
	Down	buy	Sell	Sell

meltdown, many companies downsize their workforce and impose a hiring freeze. This leads to a higher unemployment rate and hence a negative impact on the stock markets. Table 5.3 shows how investors might react to specific indicator movements.

In order to trade profitably and interpret correctly the current state of the economy, it is essential to appreciate the effects of economic indicators on the stock markets. Moreover, it will assist investors in making wise and informed decisions on whether or not to invest in the companies or indices they are interested in.

Contracts for Difference

A CFD is a derivative instrument that allows you to participate in the price movement (trade) of the underlying stock or index without owning the shares of the company. It is an agreement concerning two parties where both the parties agree that any difference between the current value of an asset at the time of accepting the agreement and the market value of the asset at the time of completing the sale will be settled by one or other party, contingent on whose favor the price is. The parties are always a seller and a buyer.

CFDs are generally used to speculate on the movement of market prices in the future irrespective of whether the underlying is appreciating or depreciating. To make money from falling prices, you can sell (go short), or to make money from rising prices, you can buy (go long). You can also use a CFD as a hedging instrument on your stock or indices trading to mitigate any potential loss of value of your investments in stocks.

Most online brokers have facilities that allow you to trade CFDs on stocks, indices, and commodities.

Advantages of CFDs

1. More flexible trading strategy—you can buy low to sell high or sell high to buy low which is something you cannot do with a normal stock account because you cannot sell stock you do not own. With a CFD you can adjust your position according to the market conditions.
2. Leverage—if, for example, you have 100 dollars to invest in a stock lot and the lot is priced at 100 dollars, you will own one lot. With a CFD however, there is a leverage of 10 or more times your investment (depending on your broker), so you can purchase multiple lots for the same level of capital. Also, you could either diversify and buy multiple lots of different shares or any combination you choose or simply purchase multiple lots of the same share.
3. Compared with the underlying markets, there are more hours of the day during which you can trade.
4. Trading CFDs means that you can increase your exposure with less initial investment, thereby enjoying a more efficient use of capital.

How Does a CFD Work?

When you are placing a trade, you can either buy a contract (going long) because you predict that the price in the underlying asset will increase over a period of time, or you sell a contract (going short) because you predict that the price in the underlying asset will fall over a period of time. The CFD price is quoted as a two-way price—bid and offer. You go long on the offer price and go short on the bid price.

The price of a CFD accurately reflects the live price of the underlying asset whether it be an individual share, a stock index value, or the price of a commodity.

Profit on Better Performance

CFDs can be traded in pairs. This is a popular way to profit on the expectation that one stock market will outperform another. To trade CFDs in pairs simply open a long position on one index and a short position on the other. It does not matter if the markets rise and fall in pair trading, only that one index outperforms the other.

Hedging

One important and critical advantage of CFDs for portfolio management is that you can hedge an existing portfolio to protect it from a falling market and any potential losses. Say you were worried that the price of the Dow would go down but you were not sure, but you did not want to sell your long position in the Dow index, you could sell a CFD to the value of the Dow position you had and if the price dropped, what you lost in price on the index you would gain on the CFD and mitigate your risk.

Typical Investment Strategy Using CFDs

Imagine that you believe that the price of XYZ shares will rise in the future and so you decide to enter into a trade to buy 5,000 XYZ shares equivalent in CFDs. The XYZ shares are priced at 675 cents bid and 676 cents offer.

Price at which shares purchased (USD)	6.76
Number of equivalent shares bought	5,000
Value of position opened in (USD)	33,800.00
Commission paid @ 0.2 percent (USD)	67.60
Margin @ 10 percent (USD)	3,380.00

A week later the price of XYZ shares reached 692 pence a share and the investor decides to cash in and sell the CFDs.

Price of XYZ shares sold (USD)	6.92
Number of equivalent shares bought	5,000
Value of position closed in (USD)	34,600.00
Commission paid @ 0.2 percent (USD)	69.20

Profit and loss on trade:

Closing value (USD)	34,600.00
Opening value (USD)	33,800.00
Less commissions paid	136.80
Profit on trade (USD)	663.20

The investor has made a profit of USD663.20 on the trade with an outlay of USD3,380 or the equivalent of 19.6 percent return on the investment.

Hedging a Position Using CFDs in Order to Protect an Investment

Say you like the look of ABC shares and decide to buy 6,000 of them. The shares are priced at 445 to 450 pence. You also decide to hedge against the price of shares falling by going short of ABC shares in CFDs at 445 pence.

Price at which shares purchased (USD)	4.50
Number of equivalent shares bought	6,000
Value of position opened in (USD)	27,000.00
Commission paid @ 0.2 percent (USD)	54.00
Total cost (USD)	27,054.00
Price of ABC shares sold in CFDs (USD)	4.45
Number of equivalent shares sold	6,000
Commission paid @ 0.20 percent (USD)	54.00
Margin requirement 10 percent (USD)	2,700.00
Total cost of hedge (USD)	2,754.00

A month later the price of ABC shares is at 425 to 430 pence, a loss of 20 pence a share, however as you had gone short on CFDs at 445 pence, you had made a gain of 20 pence a share and were therefore perfectly hedged at a cost of USD108 in commissions.

In Conclusion

Trading CFDs is a way of trading equities, indices, and other assets without a huge capital outlay. It is a simple investment as long as you keep in perspective that as with any other individual investment, not only are there potential rewards, there are also downside risks.

Options

An option is a derivative financial instrument which gives the buyer the right but not the obligation to buy the underlying asset at an agreed price (strike price), on or before an agreed date (expiration date) in the future. For this right, the buyer of the option pays a fee (the premium).

The buyer of an option can purchase a call option (right to buy the underlying asset) or a put option (right to sell the underlying asset).

The "holder" of a call option (Figure 5.2) is hoping that the underlying asset will increase in price so that the option holder can sell the option for a profit at expiration. If the underlying asset does not rise above the strike price, the holder can simply let the option expire and the maximum loss will be the premium paid. Buyers of calls are bullish on an asset, while buyers of put options are bearish on an asset. In Figure 5.2 a buyer has

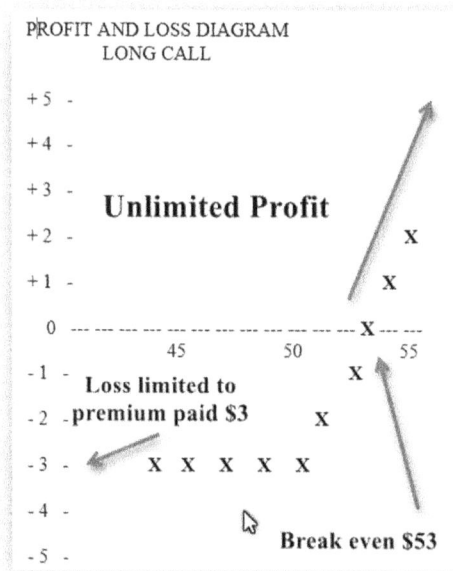

Figure 5.2 *Long call P&L diagram*

purchased a long call of ABC stock at USD50 at a premium of USD3. If the stock price stays under USD53, the option is considered to be "out of the money." If the stock price is at USD53 (breakeven), it is considered "at the money." Once the stock price is above breakeven, it is considered "in the money."

The buyer of a put option (Figure 5.3) would be expecting the price of the underlying asset (ABC stock) to fall below the strike price of USD50 and be "in the money." If it does, then the holder can sell the option at a profit. If ABC stock does not fall below the strike price, the option is "out of the money" and the option holder's only risk is the cost of the premium of USD2 which is paid to the option writer. If ABC stock is at the breakeven price of USD48 at expiry, the option is considered "at the money."

The option seller, also known as the writer of an option, can sell either a call option or a put option. Unlike the buyer (holder) of an option, the seller of the option is obliged to uphold their side of the contract. As the writer of an option cannot be sure if the option holder will exercise the option or not, the writer receives a premium from the

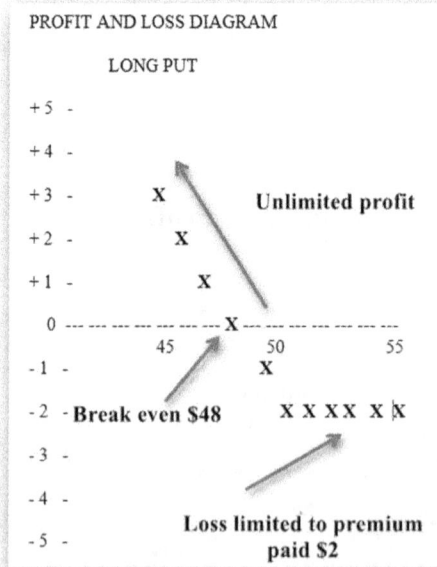

Figure 5.3 *Long put P&L diagram*

option holder for the risk he is taking. If the option holder decides to let the option expire, the premium the option writer receives is the profit. If the option holder chooses to exercise the option, then the option writers' losses could be very high, especially if the price of the underlying asset has moved a long way from the strike price.

There are several types of options available to the investor and they are categorized in classes as follows:

American type option is a term that refers to how the option is exercised. An American option can be exercised at any time during the life of the contract. It could be exercised a few days after the contract is opened or at any time before the expiration date. These options are the most used in today's markets and all the examples of options in this book are American type options.

European type option is an option that gives the option holder the right to exercise the option on the specified expiration date only. For example, you might have a European option that gives you the right to buy 100 ABC shares on 15th June at USD5.00 per share. The price rises between now and 19th May and reaches USD10.00 per share, but you cannot exercise your option until 15th June. By the time 15th June arrives, the stock is only worth USD2.00 per share. Now you will most likely let your option expire worthless.

Barrier option is an option that has a component in addition to the strike price and the expiry date. This component is called a "trigger." The trigger or barrier price if reached either opens the options contract (knocks in) and makes it a regular options contract or cancels the option contract (knocks out) and the contract is never taken up. These options are cheaper than plain vanilla options because in many cases these options never materialize.

Binary option are very simple to use and trade. The reason they are called binary or digital options is that when you trade them you only have two decisions to make, either a 0 or a 1. It is a bit like flipping a coin, you can call heads or tails, and there is no other option available to you. This is the same for the binary option; its future price is either going to be "up" or its going to be "down." What could be simpler than that? This is what makes the binary option an excellent and easy way for a novice trader to get into the global trading markets and trade currencies, stocks, commodities, or stock indices.

Exchange traded options are regulated as they are traded in an exchange. They have standardized contracts which are clearing house settled. The underlying assets for exchange traded options usually are

- Stocks (stock options)
- Commodities (options on futures)
- Bonds (interest rate options)
- Stock market index options (index options)
- Options on futures contracts
- Forex (currency options)

Over-the-counter options are options traded between two parties and are non-standardized so that the option can be tailored for any business or individual need. Most of the time one of the parties, which is usually the writer of the option, is a well-capitalized institution such as a bank or an online broker. The option types that are mainly traded over the counter are

- Stocks (stock options)
- Forex (currency options)
- Stock market (index options)
- Binary options

These are the options that you will be able to trade on an online broker's platform of your choice.

Trading Stock Options

You can trade stock options on most online brokerage platforms. As with forex trading or indeed all trading, before you trade with real money make sure that you understand the characteristics of stock options. The trading screen for a stock option will look very similar to the screen given.

In Table 5.4, let us assume that you believe that Apple shares will appreciate over time. To take advantage of this you decide to buy 100

Table 5.4 Stock option trade

Instrument	Strike price	Expiry date	Call/ put	Sell	Buy	Contracts	Contract value
Apple	USD160	18th October	Call	1.98	2.02	100	USD202.00

call option contracts at the price of USD2.02 each. The price is the premium paid. The margin payable is 20 percent which is USD40.40. So, you have effectively bought the right but not the obligation to buy 100 Apple shares before or on the 18th October. And for this right, you have paid a premium of USD202 instead of paying USD16,000 for the 100 shares. If the price of Apple shares on the 18th October is USD152 (out of the money), you let the option expire worthless and your loss is the premium paid. However, if before or on the 18th October the price of Apple shares has increased in value to say USD170 per share (in the money), you could exercise the option at the option price of USD10 per share giving you a profit of 100 × USD10 = USD1,000 less the premium you paid of USD202, leaving you with a profit of USD798 on the trade.

Table 5.5 is an example of the option exercised in the money on or before expiry. Table 5.6 is an example of the option expiring out of the money with just the loss of the premium.

Table 5.5 Stock option: trade exercised (in the money)

Instrument	Strike price	Contracts	Expiry date	Call/ put	Option price at start	Option exercise price	Profit per share
Apple	USD 160	100	18th October	Call	USD2.02	USD10	USD7.98

Table 5.6 Stock option trade (out of the money)

Instrument	Strike price	Contracts	Expiry date	Call/ put	Option price at start	Option allowed to expire	Loss is premium paid
Apple	USD160	100	18th October	Call	USD2.02	−USD8	USD202

Both the previous examples are purchases of call options and for the purchase of put options the workings would be similar except that instead of the price needing to be above the strike price to make a profit, with a put it needs to be below the strike price.

Now, what if you were the writer of the above call option and not the purchaser? As a writer, you would be hoping that the call option would expire worthless so you could pocket the premium and make a profit. However, the stock option that was exercised in the money would cost you the USD798 you would have had to pay to the purchaser of the option, less the premium of USD202 you received, leaving you with a loss of USD596.

Stock options can be used for speculation on the direction of the market as in the example above or as a hedging tool. As a hedging tool the investor who had, for example, a long stock position in ABC shares and was not sure where the market was going and did not want to sell the shares, would open a long put position to match the number of shares held. In this way, if the market went down, the loss on the shares the investor held would be matched by the gain made on the "in the money" put options. In this case, a perfect hedge. However, if the market continued to gain, all the investor would lose is the premium paid for the put options purchased.

Trading Foreign Currency Options

Currency options have the same characteristics as other options that are tradable in the markets, such as stocks. Most currency options are traded over the counter with little regulation, but a few are traded on exchanges which are highly regulated. Over-the-counter options can be traded through a broker's trading platform. Foreign currency options are slightly different from traditional options in that with traditional options you pay for the right to buy or sell a given asset, but with a currency option you buy or sell the right to money denominated in another currency.

As we have mentioned earlier, there are four positions that you can take depending on your options strategy and whether you are bullish or bearish on a particular asset (Table 5.7).

Table 5.7 Option strategy

Option type	Strategy
Buy call	Bullish
Buy put	Bearish
Sell/write put	Bullish
Sell/write call	Bearish

Long Call

For example, suppose you were bullish on the price of the USD/CAD. You buy a long call at a strike price of 1.2300 paying a premium of USD0.005/CAD with an expiry date 2 months into the future. At expiry, you will not exercise if the spot rate is below USD1.2300/CAD. You do however exercise if the spot rate is above USD1.2300/CAD. The breakeven point is at the spot rate of USD1.2350/CAD. If the spot rate is USD1.2450/CAD, you purchase the CAD at the strike price of USD1.2300/CAD and sell them on the current spot market at a rate of USD1.2450/CAD. Because you paid a premium of USD0.005/CAD, you earn a profit of USD 0.01 per CAD purchased. For this transaction, the profits can be computed as:

If the spot price was below USD1.2300 at expiry and you simply let the option expire without exercising it, you would lose the premium you paid of USD0.005/CAD. So, if, for example, you had bought 100 options (standard size 1,000 units of base currency), it would mean the premium paid would be $100 \times 1,000 \times 0.005 = £500$. As you can see, the profit potential for a long call is unlimited and the potential lose is limited to the premium paid (Table 5.8).

Table 5.8 Option long call profit calculation

Spot rate	–	Strike price + premium	=	Profit
1.2450	–	1.2300 + 0.005	=	0.01

Short Call

On the other hand, if you were the writer of this call (short call), you would be hoping that the spot rate at maturity is below the strike price. As we have seen in Table 5.7, the payoffs to the writer are the opposite of the payoff to the holder. In other words, the Premium – (Spot rate – Strike price) = Profit. Here the potential gain is limited to the premium, but the maximum loss is infinite.

Long Put

Let us look at another strategy and suppose you were bearish on the price of the USD/CAD but did not want to take the risk of entering a straightforward forex transaction and being wrong on the outcome. So, you decide to buy a USD/CAD long put. This is a bet that the spot rate at maturity is below the strike price (you are selling foreign currencies).

You purchase a put option contract on the USD/CAD at a strike price of USD1.2300/CAD (at the money option) and pay a premium of USD0.005/CAD. At maturity, you do not exercise if the spot rate is below USD1.2300/CAD. However, you do exercise if the spot rate is above USD1.2300/CAD. The breakeven point is the spot rate of USD1.2250/CAD. If the spot rate is USD1.2150/CAD, you buy the CAD on the current spot market at the rate of USD1.2150/CAD and sell them at the strike price of USD1.2300/CAD. Because you paid a premium of USD0.005/CAD, you earn a profit of USD0.01 per CAD sold. For this transaction, the profits can be computed as:

As with the long call, the potential gain is unlimited but the maximum loss is only the premium paid (Table 5.9).

Short Put

A writer of a short put however would be betting that the spot rate is above the strike price at maturity. We have seen from Table 5.7 that the

Table 5.9 Option long put profit calculation

Strike price	–	Spot rate + premium	=	Profit
1.2300	–	1.2150 + 0.005	=	0.01

payoffs to the writer are the exact opposite to the holder of a long put because the writer's profit is the premium when the option is left to expire and not exercised. That is, Premium – (Strike price – Spot rate) = Profit. As with a short call, the potential gain is limited to the premium and the maximum loss is infinite.

There are essentially only two currency option strategies you could employ:

1. Speculating on the price action of the currency spot market.
2. Hedging an open currency position.

The examples above are straightforward speculative strategies, however to hedge a position you would have to open an opposite currency option to the position you held. For example, if you held a long currency position, you would open a long put currency option to match the value of the currency position held. If your long position gained value in your favor, you would allow the long put to expire worthless, so your net profit would be the increase in value of your long position less the premium you paid for the long put. If the value of your long position fell, the loss on that position would be offset by the gains you made on your long put (see Table 5.10).

When the long call is allowed to expire because you have made a profit on your long spot position, your net profit is your spot position profit less

Table 5.10 Long call hedge

Long call allowed to expire		
Opening spot rate	**Closing spot rate**	**Profit**
EUR 1.1750/USD	EUR 1.1900/USD	EUR 0.150/USD
Long put strike price	Premium paid	Net profit
EUR 1.1750/USD	EUR 0.005/USD	**EUR/0.145/USD**
Long call exercised		
Opening spot rate	**Closing spot rate**	**Loss**
EUR 1.1750/USD	EUR 1.1500/USD	EUR 0.250/USD
Long put strike price	Premium paid	Profit
EUR 1.1750/USD	EUR 0.005/USD	EUR/0.250/USD
	Exercise price	Profit less premium paid
	EUR 1.1500	**EUR 0.245/USD**

the premium paid. If the long call is exercised, then the profit on the call offsets the loss on your long position and your cost is the premium paid.

Trading Stock Index Options

Index options are the same as a stock option, except the underlying asset is an index instead of a stock. Exactly like an equity call option, an index call option is the right to buy the underlying index. Similarly, just like an equity put option, an index put option is the right to sell the underlying index. As we have previously discussed, the difference between calls and puts is that the owner of an index call option has the right to buy an index at a certain price. The owner of a put option has the right to sell an index at a certain price. Once owned, you have the choice of whether you want to exercise the option and take a position on the underlying asset or simply let them expire worthless if the current market index price is less than the strike price for a call or the market price is more than the strike price for a put.

Most online broker platforms facilitate the trading of stock index options and you should choose the one that meets your own personal trading goals. The platforms that facilitate index options normally have the major stock indices as tradable assets, although some do allow trading the lesser indices. The most popular indices for trading options are shown in Table 5.11.

Table 5.11 Popular indices

Index	Country
Standard and Poor's 500	USA
Dow Jones 30	USA
NASDAQ	USA
FTSE 100	UK
DAX	Germany
Hang Seng	Hong Kong
CAC 40	France
Nikkei 500	Japan
FTSE MID 250	UK
Russel 3000	USA

Table 5.12 Index options screenshot

Index	Strike price	Expiry date	Put/call	Sell/write premium	Buy premium
SPX	2,480	Oct	Call	35.72	36.52
SPX	2,480	Oct	Put	14.59	15.16
SPX	2,490	Oct	Call	28.20	28.80
SPX	2,490	Oct	Put	16.92	17.57
SPX	2,500	Oct	Call	24.08	25.41
SPX	2,500	Oct	Put	14.48	15.56

Take a look at an example of a typical trading platform's index option screen in Table 5.12.

The first column shows index option SPX which is the designation for the underlying asset Standard and Poor's Index. The second column shows an array of strike prices. The third column is the expiry month for the option. The fourth column designates whether the strike price is for a put or a call. The fifth column is the premium on the sell/write side of the option. The sixth column indicates the premium on the buy side of the option.

Index Option Long Call Example

You observe that the current value of the S&P 500 is at the 2,490 level. You believe that the index will rise over the next weeks so you decide to buy a long call SPX with a strike price as near to the current price as possible. You choose the strike price of 2,500 which has a premium of USD25.41 and an expiry date in October a few weeks from now. With a contract multiplier of USD100, the premium you have to pay to hold the call option is USD2,541. On the expiration date, the underlying S&P 500 index has risen by 5 percent and stood at 2614.50. With the S&P Index significantly higher than the strike price, the option is very much in the money. You exercise the option and receive a cash settlement figure that is computed as follows: (2614.50 − 2500) × USD100 = USD11,450 from the option transaction. Deduct the premium of USD2,541 and your net profit is USD8,909 from the long call strategy. As with the settling of all option contracts, it is not necessary to exercise the option to take your profit, you can simply close out the option by selling it back into the market.

The obvious advantage from the long call strategy is that your loss is limited to a known specific amount but your profits are unlimited. If the S&P 500 had fallen by 5 percent to 2,375 instead of rising, which is a long way from the strike price of 2,500, you would have only lost USD2,541, the cost of your premium paid.

A long put strategy on the same index option would work in exactly the same way as the long call strategy except that you would want to see the underlying asset fall below the strike price to make a profit. If the underlying asset rose above the strike price, you would lose the premium you had paid. Writing or selling put and call index options exposes you to the possibility of unlimited losses if you get it wrong. Recall that when writing or selling a put index option, your expectation is that the underlying asset will rise above the strike price. Conversely, when writing a call index option you are expecting the underlying price to fall below the strike price.

Keep in mind that long call or put strategies can lead to unlimited profits but limited losses if you get it wrong and short call or put strategies can lead to limited profits and but unlimited losses if the market goes against you.

Binary Options

Binary options are nothing like the options we have been talking about in this chapter. They are much simpler to use and trade. The reason they are called binary or digital options is that when you trade them you only have two decisions to make, either a 0 or a 1. It is a bit like flipping a coin, you can call heads or tails, and there is no other option available to you. This is the same for the binary option; its future price is either going to be "up" or its going to be "down." What could be simpler than that? This is what makes the binary option an excellent and easy way for you as a novice to get into the trading global markets, trading currencies, stocks, commodities, or stock indices.

The key to the functionality of a binary option is that it is known as a "fixed return option." In other words, unlike other forms of trading products, you will know before you trade what your exact profit or loss will be. Therefore, however much the price of the asset you are trading has moved

https://www.binary.com/en/trading.html?
underlying=frxEURUSD&currency=USD&market=forex&formname=risefall&date_start=now&duration_amount=1&duration_units=d&
expiry_type=duration&amount=1&amount_type=stake

Figure 5.4 Binary options screenshot

in your favor, you will always receive a predetermined fixed amount of profit, around 70 percent of your initial investment amount. So, you can invest USD100 and if you are correct in your prediction you get USD170 back. Similarly, no matter how wrong you are, your loss will be around 100 percent of your investment amount. If you invest USD100 and get it wrong, you will get back USD0. I expect you are thinking that trading binary options sounds like a lottery. However, it is not, you can take most of the luck out of trading these types of options, as with all types, by using technical analysis tools, reading the financial press and following the economic calendar. All these tools are available on most binary option trading platforms and as with the MT4, with just a few clicks you are able to choose candlesticks, moving averages, stochastics, time frames, and popular indicators to populate the trading screen. The given screenshot is typical of a broker's binary option online platform (Figure 5.4).

High/Low Trading

The simplest binary option to trade is to use the high/low tactic because it has many similarities to tossing a coin. All you need to do is select an asset you want to trade, say EUR/USD (see above graphic) and you speculate that at a certain point in the future, the price of the EUR/USD currency pair will be higher (call option) or lower (put option) than the current price. If you predicted higher and at the expiry time, the price of the EUR/USD currency pair is higher than the current price, you make a profit from the trade and receive a predetermined amount of money, usually 70 percent of your investment. However, if, at the expiry time, the price of the EUR/USD currency pair is below the current price, you make a loss and would lose all your investment. Similarly, if you predicted the price of the EUR/USD would be lower than the current price at the expiry time and you were right, you make a profit. If you were wrong, you make a loss. You are able to select from a whole array of expiry times or dates from 5 seconds to 60 days or more ahead.

One Touch Trading

With the "one touch" tactic instead of predicting that the price of the EUR/USD currency pair will be higher or lower than the current price at expiry, you predict that at some time before the expiry time, the price of EUR/USD will touch a specific strike price. If the price of EUR/USD reached your target strike price before your selected time frame had expired, even for a brief moment, you would make a profit. If it did not touch your selected strike price before the binary option had expired, you would make a loss. For example, suppose the current EUR/USD price was 1.1700 and you had a choice of strike prices and expiry dates at 1.1500/3 days – 1.1550/2 days – 1.1600/1 day – 1.1750/1 day – 1.1800/2 days – 1.1850/2 days. You believe that the current bearish trend will continue and you choose a strike price of 1.1600 with expiry in 1 day. If the EUR/USD price reaches 1.1600 before the expiry time, you win. If not, you lose.

Touch—No Touch Trading

A variation of the one touch tactic, using this tactic you can either predict that a strike price will be reached as in the one touch tactic, or, you predict that a strike price will not be reached before the expiry date. For example, if we take the same array of strike prices and expiry dates as in our one touch example, 1.1500/3 days – 1.1550/2 days – 1.1600/1 day – 1.1750/1 day – 1.1800/2 days – 1.1850/2 days, instead of predicting that the EUR/USD price will touch 1.1600 before expiry, you predict that the EUR/USD price would not touch the 1.1600 strike price before expiry.

Range Trading

In the range trading tactic, you predict whether the price of say Google stock would finish either outside or inside a certain price range. So, for example, if Google stock was currently trading at USD784 and you selected "inside" a price range of USD782.80 to USD789.50, and if at the selected expiry the price of Google was USD788.30, you would make a profit. If the price was above USD789.50 or below USD782.80 you would make a loss. Range trading usually has a fixed return around the 80 percent range to reflect the difficulty of this particular tactic.

For novice traders, the attraction of binary options is the entry capital. There are many brokers who accommodate binary options trades of USD1. This enables you to start trading with real money in the stock, commodities, currency, and stock index markets, but if you lose you are not going to lose your shirt. After all, winning a binary options trade with a capital of USD1 gives you a profit of 70 to 80 cents each time you win. Another reason that binary options are popular is that most people prefer straightforward decisions where the result is known within minutes or hours and not in days or weeks, although, on some platforms it is possible to trade up to 60 days into the future.

CHAPTER 6

Tips for Successful Trading Strategies

Developing a profitable trading plan will enable you to be more successful in getting out of bad trades or staying in good trades. It is possible with a fully developed trading plan to have established the optimum buy and sell triggers and entry points that offer the highest probability of large profits. Your trading system should reflect the markets (currency, commodity, index, or stock) that you feel comfortable trading and the leverage you consider the optimum you need. For example, if you trade the EUR/USD, you will need to decide if you are going to trade a 1:10, 1:50, 1:100, or 1:200 leverage and make sure these parameters are in your trading system. In order to configure your trading software, there are some key steps to complete:

1. Write down in detail your thought processes in coming to a decision on your entry and exit points.
2. Define the currencies which you want to trade and write down the analysis on how you arrived at the decision. This applies to your decisions on optimum leverage, trade entry/exit points, markets, stops, and take-profit pips. This should be done for all markets and assets you trade.
3. Test your plan on a trading platform demo account before you go live.
4. Compile a list of self-discipline rules, including money management, similar to the tips that I have detailed later in this chapter.

The trading plan might seem like a lot of work for little gain, but believe me it is worth spending time getting your trading plan right, otherwise you will find yourself struggling to make successful trades. Too many unsuccessful trades erode your self-confidence and leads down the path to losing your allotted trading capital and giving up.

Trading as a Business—Successful Trading Principles

Currency trading or any trading in fact is not a matter of putting on a magician's hat and waving a wand; some traders can make accurate market predictions, but in the end, that is all they are. A prediction is not a sound way to make money trading. The sound way to make money trading is to trade correctly. Trading correctly is above all having the discipline to keep to a trading strategy whatever the results of the previous trade. Even the most successful traders and gurus of our times did not make money on their predictions; they made money from keeping to a proper trading strategy. Remember that trading is not a game, it is a business, therefore a trader must use sound business techniques to be successful.

One of the soundest principles of any trading strategy is controlling risk through managing capital. As in any other business, even if the product is the latest and greatest, if the business does not control its costs, allocate its capital in an efficient manner, and does not have a viable business strategy, the business will eventually fail. The number-one rule of thumb is to never second guess your own strategy and never tweak your own indicators so they meet your strategy criteria.

Risk management is key and that should be uppermost in your mind. Trading is like any other business. If the demand is there, you buy, if the demand is not there, you sell. If you had a diner and there was a big demand for fish and chips, would you serve eggs and bacon? No of course not. So, when the market is up, the trader should be long and when the market is down the trader should be short. Never ever go against the market. If you start fighting the market you are going to lose your capital very quickly. Follow the market and the market will give you more profits than the losses it takes from you. Keep in mind that there is no such thing as a trader who is right 100 percent of the time. If you are right 60 percent of the time then you have a sound business.

You should not be impatient to make money and focus just on short-term profits. Be in it for the long haul. If your trading strategy is sound, it will give you profits over time and not just tomorrow or next week, but in the months ahead. Do not take profits too early because you have let your fears and emotions take over. Let the market tell you when it is time to take a profit.

Always accept your losses and do not dwell on them. Treat them as the cost of running your business. Successful traders make a lot of losing trades, so do not be afraid of the losses. Let the market make its moves, and if your strategy is sound you will make money in the long term.

Risk Management

A crucial and essential prerequisite for successful trading which is often ignored by new traders is managing risk. Many times this is due to the fact that new traders fail to distinguish between speculation and gambling. When speculating you have some form of control over risk, whereas in gambling, the casinos or bookmakers always hold the advantage. To be able to make money consistently you have to know how to manage risk. The risk you run when trading is that you will lose the capital you have invested in the trade. If you trade without regard for the risk you are taking on, or without any money management system in place, you might as well be in a casino and gamble your money away.

As we have seen in previous chapters, it is vitally important that you gain a good grounding in both technical analysis and fundamental analysis. Trading platforms are packed with all the necessary technical analysis tools that you need. Most trading platforms also provide access to the economic calendar and have some form of ticker that announces the latest financial news.

A key question you need to answer when you start out trading is "how much capital do I need to get started?" Money creates money, so obviously you are going to have to set aside an amount of capital with which to start trading. Whether you start trading on a micro, mini, or regular account, your money management techniques should be the same.

The key to risk management is deciding on how much you are willing to risk losing on any one trade. There is not a trader on the planet who achieves 100 percent winning trades. So, you are going to lose some trades and sometimes you could lose several trades in a row, so it is vital that you manage your risk. If the percentage of the trade that you risk losing is too high, say 10 percent per trade and you start with a capital of USD10,000, a losing streak of five trades in a row will reduce your capital by half. However, if your risk management is conservative and you only risk 2 percent of your capital per trade, a losing streak of five trades only loses you 10 percent of your capital. The key is to set up your risk management so that you are protected from a bad series of drawdowns. Bear in mind that to regain 40 percent of lost capital, your percentage win rate needs to be around the 70 percent mark. That is the reason you have to protect your account because it is much harder to win back the money you have lost.

In addition to computing the odds of a successful trade, it is vital that you decide before you enter a trade at which point you will pull out of the trade. In other words, at which point will you be happy with the profit you have made. The difference between the cut-off point and your entry point is the trade's level of risk. You can manage this risk by using a "take-profit" trigger price. This is an order to your broker to close the trade when the price of the asset has reached a certain level.

Another key risk management tool is the "stop-loss" trigger. This is an order to your broker to close the trade when the price reaches a level of loss that you are not willing to surpass. This limits your overall losses. Your risk management strategy could, for example, be that you set all stop losses at a certain percentage of the capital you employed on the trade.

The key to successful trading is to know exactly when you are going to enter and exit a trade. So it is very important that you always remember to use a "stop loss" to limit your losses and a "take-profit" price to ensure you do not lose your profits.

Trading as a Business—A Winning Strategy Profile

As a business person, you have to develop and market your own winning strategy profile. This should be based on your skills, knowledge, and personality. The essential ingredient for this is the market condition as well as the trader behind the specific strategy. As a business person however, you need to keep in mind that these are not created in a vacuum. Rather you have to understand the environment you intend to apply them and whether they work or not. When trading, keep in mind that one size does not fit all. There are some strategies that will work on one thing and not another and for this reason, finding the best strategy for a specific business is important. The financial markets for instance are volatile in nature and extremely dynamic and it is for this reason that as a trader, it is important for you to have a specific trading strategy. Understanding the market landscape is what a successful winning strategy is all about and it also makes it easier to come up with a set of profit goals and a comfortable risk tolerance. To accomplish this however, it is important to understand how to evaluate available trading strategies, understand the market, and develop and test the different trading strategies.

As we have seen in earlier chapters, there are essentially only three market conditions and these conditions form three diverse chart patterns which reflect the market action. These three conditions are classed as a volatile or a directionless or a trending market.

The characteristics of a volatile market (see Figure 6.1) are very sharp changes in price both up and down. If you were to trade in volatile market conditions, you would be out of the market most of the time as your trades should be short lived and designed to make small profits per trade.

A directionless or ranging market, on the other hand, shows a price range that has very narrow price movements between highs and lows.

Figure 6.1 *Volatility price chart*

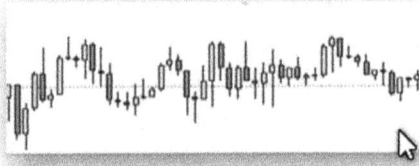

Figure 6.2 Ranging market

The trading strategy for trading in such a market is what is called swing trading where you would calculate the support and resistant points on a price chart. You would sell when a resistance point was hit, and buy when a support point was reached (Figure 6.2).

A trending market is one in which the price chart is one directional either showing an upward trend or a downward trend. Your strategy here would be to stay in the market and take a position according to the prevailing trend and keep the position until the trend turns (Figure 6.3).

You should choose the strategy that is best for your temperament. However, it is worth bearing in mind that most successful traders use trend following strategies.

Figure 6.3 Trending market

How to Control Your Trading Emotions

It is common knowledge that over 90 percent of traders consistently lose money. How is this possible when they trade in the most liquid and volatile market on the planet? The short answer is fear, aggression, anger, greed, hope, and timidity—all emotions that are not conducive to clear level-headed thinking. To be successful you need to banish these emotions, as you would banish demons. If you are fearful, you will become afraid to lose and will gradually start to move away from your trading strategy and begin to execute actions that are outside your trading plan, in so doing you will start to lose more and more of your capital. Do not lose patience with the market and close out a position before it hits your stop loss. Hopefully, the trading plan you created has a strategic reason for you putting the stop loss where it is. If you close out before it hits and then the market moves in your direction, you will lose your confidence pretty quickly.

Trading on hope puts you in the realm of the gambler who puts money on a roulette wheel number hoping it will come up. Do not hope a bad trade will get better because it invariably would not, as that is what it is, a bad trade. Do not hope that a good trade gone bad will come back into your favor, just exit the trade and look at your trading strategy and analyze what went wrong.

Avoid being greedy by overtrading or risking more than you should of your capital, especially when the market is going your way. If your trading plan specifies 2 percent of your capital per trade, keep to it whatever the market conditions. Pay attention to what the charts are showing you and on the fundamentals and avoid overtrading.

Strong emotions can be detrimental to making money and being a successful trader. How can you suppress these emotions?

First, do not take high risks by trading more of your capital than you should. A rule of thumb is to not risk more than 5 percent of your capital on any one trade. If you keep to that rule, there is no chance of losing all your capital. As we have mentioned earlier, make a plan and stick to it. Make yourself a set of rules and keep to them. For example, if you have a rule which says that your risk reward ratio is 1:2 or 1:3, then keep to it.

You would be surprised how many traders reverse their risk reward ratios. Never overtrade as trading too much does not win you more money, all it does is cause you to risk more. Knowing when not to trade is just as important as knowing when to trade. It is also important to bear in mind that the trend is always your friend, so trading in the direction of the market and not against it is a much better way to trade.

Finally, keep a dairy of what you do, so that you discipline yourself to record what you did when you traded successfully or what you did when the trade went bad. In this way, you stay disciplined and honor your trading plan as well as eliminate those nasty niggling emotions. Happy Trading!

Trading Glossary

Bear Market – A market distinguished by falling prices.

Bid – The price level at which an asset is sold.

Bull Market – A market dominated by rising prices.

CAC – The top 40 companies listed in the Paris Stock Exchange weighted by market capitalization.

Commission – The fee charged for buying or selling securities.

Contract Size – The notional amount of shares/indices/commodities/currency controlled by a CFD or options position.

DAX – An index of the top 30 companies listed in the Frankfurt Stock Exchange weighted by market capitalization.

Dividend – The element of a company's earnings which is distributed to shareholders either bi-annually or annually. For stock, CFDs dividends are a cash modification to the account. Long position holders are credited, whereas short position holders are debited the dividend.

Dow Jones Industrial Average – An index of the 30 largest blue-chip companies listed in the United States which are price weighted.

Expiration/Expiry – A fixed duration such as option or forward contracts which expire at a predetermined date and time in the future.

FTSE 100 – An index of the top 100 companies listed in the London Stock Exchange weighted by market capitalization.

Hedge – A position that is created to specifically reduce or eliminate risk due to an unfavorable movement in price.

Interest – Charges on loans and financial instruments that reflect their risk profile.

Leverage – Leverage is the ratio of the size of the position to the amount of the deposit. It permits traders to obtain a big exposure with a moderately small outlay.

Margin – The amount required from a client to cover losses when a price moves adversely.

Market capitalization – A company's market value calculated by the current share price times the number of issued shares.

NASDAQ – The second largest stock exchange in the United States which traditionally lists many technology companies.

Nikkei 225 – An index of the top 225 shares listed in the Tokyo Stock Exchange weighted by price.

Offer – The price level at which you can buy a financial asset.

Position – An open trade.

Realized Profit/Loss – The amount of money you have made or lost on a position once it has been closed.

Sector – A selection of company stocks within a particular industry group. More often than not an index is available to track industry groups.

Settlement – Closing a position at a predetermined market price once the market is closed.

S&P 500 – An index of the top 500 companies listed in the New York Stock Exchange (NYSE) weighted by market capitalization.

Spread – The difference between the buying and selling price of a financial instrument.

Stock Exchange – A market on which securities are traded.

Stock Index – A collection of several stocks expressed as a total price and measured against a value which has a base on a specified date in the past.

Underlying – The actual traded market or markets from which the price of a futures or option is derived.

Volatility – A measure in the change of price movements of a market over a period of time.

About the Author

Philip Cooper was born and educated in the United Kingdom. He joined Citibank in London before moving to Athens where he worked as a foreign exchange trader for both Citibank and Chase Manhattan. Philip was then posted to Citibank's Middle East North African Training Centre in Athens/Beirut as the operations manager and a foreign exchange trainer. After returning to the United Kingdom, Philip joined Union Bank of Switzerland (UBS) as the head of learning and development and introduced trading simulations as a safe way for new traders to trade. In 1993, he was appointed head of learning and education for UBS in North America, specifically to develop simulations and interactive training programs on the financial markets. He later left the bank and went into partnership with two colleagues to set up a successful financial training company (New Learning Developments) in New York City. At New Learning Developments, he developed relationships with all the major investment and international banks in New York and Chicago, including Goldman, Lehman, JP Morgan, and other major financial institutions such as The Federal Reserve Bank and the World Bank. In 1999, he returned to London where he worked as a training consultant to financial services institutions and the Ministry of Defence. During 2007–2015, he was involved in developing knowledge databases for some of the most prominent online brokerage houses on the Internet. Currently, he is working on his first novel and another financial book on options.

Index

OTHER TITLES IN OUR FINANCE AND FINANCIAL MANAGEMENT COLLECTION

John A. Doukas, Old Dominion University, *Editor*

- *Rethinking Risk Management: Critically Examining Old Ideas and New Concepts* by Rick Nason
- *Towards a Safer World of Banking: Bank Regulation After the Subprime Crisis* by T.T. Ram Mohan
- *The Penny Share Millionaire: The Ultimate Guide to Trading* by Jacques Magliolo
- *Escape from the Central Bank Trap: How to Escape From the $20 Trillion Monetary Expansion Unharmed* by Daniel Lacalle
- *Applied International Finance Volume I, Second Edition: Managing Foreign Exchange Risk* by Thomas J. O'Brien
- *Tips & Tricks for Excel-Based Financial Modeling, Volume I: A Must for Engineers & Financial Analysts* by M.A. Mian
- *Tips & Tricks for Excel-Based Financial Modeling, Volume II: A Must for Engineers & Financial Analysts* by M.A. Mian
- *The Anti-Bubbles: Opportunities Heading into Lehman Squared and Gold's Perfect Storm* by Diego Parrilla
- *Applied International Finance Volume II, Second Edition: International Cost of Capital and Capital Budgeting* by Thomas J. O'Brien
- *Hypocrisy of the African Public Finance Management Framework: The Case of Malawi* by Kamudoni Nyasulu
- *Welcome to My Trading Room, Volume II: Basics to Trading Global Shares, Futures, and Forex: Create Your Own Brokerage* by Jacques Magliolo
- *Welcome to My Trading Room, Volume III: Basics to Trading Global Shares, Futures, and Forex–Advanced Methodologies and Strategies* by Jacques Magliolo
- *Enterprise Risk Management in a Nutshell* by Dennis Cox
- *Venture Capital Networks: A Multi-Level Perspective* by Cristiano Bellavitis

Announcing the Business Expert Press Digital Library

Concise e-books business students need for classroom and research

This book can also be purchased in an e-book collection by your library as

- a one-time purchase,
- that is owned forever,
- allows for simultaneous readers,
- has no restrictions on printing, and
- can be downloaded as PDFs from within the library community.

Our digital library collections are a great solution to beat the rising cost of textbooks. E-books can be loaded into their course management systems or onto students' e-book readers. The **Business Expert Press** digital libraries are very affordable, with no obligation to buy in future years. For more information, please visit **www.businessexpertpress.com/librarians**. To set up a trial in the United States, please email **sales@businessexpertpress.com**.